His Eye is On the Sparrow

A Memoir

by Elenita J.

MOF Publishing

MOF PUBLISHING

MOF PUBLISHING

MOF Publishing

His Eye is on the Sparrow: A Memoir

paperback edition © March 2017: ISBN 978-0-9958951-2-6

Requests for information should be addressed to:
MOF Publishing
mofpublishing@proinbox.com

Library and Archives Canada Cataloguing in Publication
J., Elenita, 1961-, author
His eye is on the sparrow : a memoir / by Elenita J.

Issued in print and electronic formats.
ISBN 978-0-9958951-2-6 (softcover).--ISBN 978-0-9958951-0-2(HTML).--
ISBN 978-0-9958951-1-9 (HTML)

1. J., Elenita, 1961-. 2. Parents--Death. 3. Grief.
4. Autobiographies. I. Title.

BF575.G7J3 2017 155.9'37 C2017-902425-6
C2017-902426-4

Cover design: Elenita J. and T. & J. Normandeau
Interior design & composition: Elenita J.
Printed in Canada

Table of Contents

Acknowledgements	vi
Introduction	vii
Prologue: To Survive is not Enough	1
Snakes in the Banana Grove	4
The Weeping Trees	16
Wind in the Curtains	27
Red Linoleum	36
The Orange Cassette Player	43
Those Last Words	48
Goodbye Pepsi	53
Holding My Breath	58
My Australian Friends	64
She Sings for Me	74
The Singing Bird	80
A Boatload of Barnacles	84
Humpty Meets the King	90
Another Child, Another Mother	99
The Ball of Wax	104
39 Days from 12	111
A Terrible Movie	117
Crackling Voices	121
Red Ruby Cloak	126
A Green, Happy Place	136
The Artist's Studio	140
The Maze	149

Treasured	153
Appendices	161
Letters	161
Dear Janet	162
Dear Ellen	172
Dear Vincent	174
References to Scriptures	179
Hymns	183
And Can it Be?	183
His Eye is on the Sparrow	184
By and By, When I Look on His Face	186
Resources	187
About the Author	189

For AJ, who is my anchor when I flail in the storms —and holds the string when my kite catches the wind.

And for my children, who despite my many shortcomings, have loved me and filled my heart with hope and joy.

Acknowledgements

I could not have written this without help. It came in the form of friends who read what I'd written when I had no strength to edit it—and said it was worth continuing. I appreciate each one who read a sliver, a slice, or the whole round pizza...and said, "Keep going."

And I needed Anna. We shared this journey in silence for the longest of years. And now as we've shared the words, she gave me eyes to see things with a little less blur. Sometimes she corrected a memory, just slightly, and made it clearer. And sometimes she said, "Leave that word out." And it became a better narrative. And she listened to the cassette with me and I was able to keep breathing. I could not have written this, or lived it, without her.

And God sent Val. A gift. A sweet, kind, generous soul who saw the worth, and then refined it with such care.

For those who have helped get this book into the hands of readers—Gail, Betty, Sharon, Sandra, Nancy, Heather, Tami, Sheri, Donny, Ama, Rose, Grace, John, Debbie, Kai, Alice, Pam, Kim, Mattie, Ginette, Melodie, Matt, Robyn, Lisa, Brenda.

Introduction

Sometimes a story that fascinates or startles us penetrates our childhood. The element of surprise creates a stronger memory, and the images of the story are imprinted within us.

The story of Pandora's Box is such a story for me. I spent my third grade in three different schools. One of those teachers told the Greek myth of Pandora and her box.

This is the story the way I remember hearing it:

The gods give Pandora a box, an urn actually, instructing her not to open it. Since we call it Pandora's Box, my image of it is a square, black box with some faded Grecian paintings under the lacquered finish.

The pressure builds inside of Pandora until she can no longer contain her curiosity, and she opens the box. Immediately a flood of evil escapes, and she quickly tries to replace the lid.

It is too late. Like a cloud of black smoke, the contents of her box have escaped. I imagine the forces of darkness swirling into the paradise she has enjoyed. Evil has invaded her world and there is nothing she can do to regain her innocence.

I am left with this image: sometimes life tumbles out of control and a dark haze swirls around us. And there is nothing we can do to solve that problem or return life to its previous bliss.

There is something I do not hear my teacher say, or have simply forgotten. Pandora's Box is not left completely empty. One thing does not escape and remains with her.

And that is hope.

Hope. For a long time, I did not see it in my box. I did not even realize it was there.

But it was.

Prologue: To Survive is not Enough

Even if you didn't experience a devastating loss as a child, there is a good chance you know someone who did. They may not look like someone who suffered a trauma; they probably look completely normal, functioning in a typical way in an ordinary life. But those who look and sound and behave convincingly normal may hide a terrible hole, a black chasm in their soul, where they lost and suffered and learned to live in the silence of that tragedy—because no one knew how to join them.

Everyone has a story to tell, and this is mine.

It isn't that my suffering is more important or greater than someone else's. It certainly isn't that it has done more damage or deserves greater attention. It might be that the outlines are sharper and the memories are clearer. Inside me they are like shards—memory shards, sharpened by the traumatic nature of the loss. It is likely that I suppressed more pain and anguish than many children. You may or may not relate.

It has now been 40 years since my mom's sudden death, a few weeks before I turned twelve. I've come through nearly fifteen years of healing, and I am almost ready to talk about it. Almost. I am aware that talking about it is part of the healing. It's likely that I'm living in the middle of that cliché from the song—"We've only just begun!"

I can write things down now that I am still unable to say aloud. Some of these things I have never told anyone. The reason for that silence is not unique to me. Silence masquerades as your best friend when you experience significant loss as a child. I don't really want to talk about generalities. I am not an expert on anyone or anything except my own story. So that is what I will tell.

In order to survive the pain of my loss, I buried it. In my silence, I created a deep hole and concealed my sorrow there.

I believed I had to. I was afraid the pain was killing me. It even felt physical, like I could be breathing my last breath. The only way to survive was to discipline myself to silence, both inside and out, and eventually to carry on as if the sorrow didn't exist.

This is my process, or part of it. I want to be clear on this: I have not found a short or easy journey for healing. As far as I can tell, there are no shortcuts; for me it has been fifteen years of allowing some leakage of that pain, each time gaining ground. I have allowed the emotions of loss to come to the surface in bits and pieces, not continuously. In those intervals, I have found healing. In the lulls between times of pain, I have sometimes believed the wound was mainly cured. It always surprised me when a new level of sorrow surfaced.

This last interval has been unique. I've allowed my heart to sink down into the sadness instead of letting it bubble to the surface. It is scary. I wonder if I am on the brink of depression. I stew in worry that if I am honest with this pain, I will fall into a pit. I will never get out. This fear is another barrier to my healing.

But I know this: as a child, I could not talk about this pain. I believed it had to be avoided, or it would have consumed me. Like Pandora's Box, there was so much darkness hidden inside, that opening up the lid felt dangerous—like the pain would destroy me. There was also my belief that if I let the darkness out of the box, I would never be able to get it back under control.

As a young adult, I felt guilty for the pain. Well-meaning listeners told me I needed to get over my mom's death. I believed them, and so I tried even harder. Ask any counsellor: this was the wrong thing for them to say and the wrong thing for me to do.

As I heard this message and reburied the pain, I prolonged the inevitable. It was the worst possible choice, for it was burying toxins that were like a volcano when they finally surfaced. It was the damage of those toxins that pushed me to get help and healing.

For now, as I reflect on my losses, I am just saying this:

You don't need to know about me—that's not my point in writing this. But I need to know about me. In order to be the person I was created to be, I need to know about me. And you, likewise, need to know about you. So if I can help you know yourself and tell your story (or be a part of someone else's story), then that is the grace I live by and invite you to enter.

Silence helps us survive, but the talking, the crying, and the connecting with each other—these are precious gifts that move us from surviving to living. And I hope we can all go on living.

Surviving is not enough.

⁂ Snakes in the Banana Grove ⁂

▪ ▪ ▪ ▪ ▪

My parents were from two different worlds—my mom came from a Mennonite family of first generation immigrants to Canada. Although they were ethnically of Mennonite background, it was a rejected part of her identity which we never spoke of. But Mennonite values of frugality, hard work, and hospitality were evident in our home. She was fiercely loyal and supportive of my dad, with his unique personality and gifts.

My dad came from New Zealand—an odd combination of old-school British culture and a newly formed nation. Innovative and conservative at the same time. There were some things that were strictly the way they were supposed to be, never changing—like how we spent our time on Sundays. There was no place for fun and entertainment on Sundays, it was strictly a serious day of rest —unless you counted my dad's hour before church time, when he pulled out sheet music and played the piano with no restraint.

Our family of four moved to Bolivia in South America when I was nearly three years old, and my sister Anna was four. It was a long boat ride from New Zealand, followed by a short plane ride from Peru. We lived in or near the city of Cochabamba for three years, starting out with a year when my parents studied Spanish in language school. My memories begin with the first year in Cochabamba.

While my parents were studying, the kitchen staff at the mission home cared for me and one other child with gentle warmth. When they heard my mom calling me "Ellen," they gave me the nickname "Elenita." This stuck with me throughout my years in elementary school, and my name, in this diminutive form, gave me a feeling of being treasured. I had touchable fine blonde curls and little round cheeks, so whenever we went out in public I had my cheeks affectionately pinched. The annoyance of being pinched balanced the warmth and goodwill feeling I got from my local name, Elenita. I eventually learned to dodge other pedestrians on the street.

The next two years my parents lived at a boarding school just outside the city of Cochabamba. Anna started school, and I lived the life of a carefree preschooler. I spent my time making sandcastles and riding my red scooter around and around the courtyard, waiting for recess and after school when friends could come out to play with me. My mom was busy, but always available nearby, and the kitchen staff enjoyed my chatting with them while they peeled tubs of vegetables, prepared for the hungry school kids. As far as I could tell, I was part of a big, happy family, though the boys were sometimes tempted to tease me with cruel tricks—swinging a snake in my face and getting me to eat a horrible tasting leaf, which turned out badly for them when they discovered it was poisonous!

After three years in the city of Cochabamba, our family moved to the jungle during the school break before I started grade one. My dad took over the tasks of flying services (food, mail, medicine) to various missionaries in remote towns isolated by miles of unperturbed jungle. In order to do this job, we moved to a small town where, surrounded by the jungle, we lived without electricity, plumbing, or motorized vehicles. We lived in a house built by the pilot who had served there before us.

We arrived on a DC-3 airplane after a long, uncomfortable flight. The DC-3 came to our town once a week, bringing people and supplies. The seats inside ran along each edge of the airplane—hard wooden seats, no padding, and no seatbelts. It was a relief and delight to get to our new home, though it did not delight my mom as much as it did me!

We lived next to the *pista*, a grassy strip of levelled ground for the DC-3 to land on. Instead of a garage we had a hangar, for the mission-owned Cessna. In our large front yard there was a small shed and a well. Inside the front door was the *sala*, our main living room. Like in everyone else's *sala*, there were two limp hammocks hanging in this room. To either side of the *sala* were the bedrooms. Straight ahead, behind the *sala* was a long narrow room that ran the width of the house with big windows looking over our back yard, a citrus grove where giant sweet grapefruit and oranges hung off the trees in an abundant supply. I stood in one of the big screened windows each morning to watch for the birds. We were serenaded regularly by a red-breasted bird that was some jungle variety of a parakeet. It was something beautiful to look forward to each morning.

We arrived in winter so the temperatures were less intense, though winter and summer were both hot. Two seasons only: hot and hotter. We needed no blankets, but a cool shower would have been nice. Instead of a bathroom, we had an outhouse out back and a bathing room in a lean-to on one side of our house. We had to pull water up from the well if we wanted to take a bath. In fact, we pulled up water for everything, and boiled it before drinking it. We had a kerosene fridge and there ended our luxuries.

Each evening at dusk bats would fly out from the rafters where they lived in all the houses, including ours. Their daily migration to the jungle was to eat fruit all night. The jungle began on the other side of the *pista*, but we never crossed the strip of land to check it out. It looked dark and dangerous and though I had an adventurous spirit, that did not tempt me.

When the bats flew out in a black cloud to eat fruit, the town generator would start up and provide enough electricity for one lightbulb hanging in the middle of each home. Ours was in the *sala*, where we rarely spent our time, so it wasn't much use. Instead my dad would put a new "mantle" in the kerosene lantern and light it. I loved to watch the netting of the mantle catch fire and then glow inside the lamp. This was a brighter light for our evening activities and had the additional benefit of being portable for our evening trip to the outhouse—I did not like going out there in the dark.

On Sunday evenings we took our lamp to church with us and hung it high on the post in the middle of that thatched building. Not everyone in town had a lantern, and ours made reading the hymnal possible. In New Zealand, my dad had been the town organist, playing a huge pipe organ for special occasions. In this jungle setting, he was an enthusiastic village organist, playing his way through the hymnal on a fold-up organ that he pumped with his feet.

The floor of our house was hard brick, which was much harder than linoleum—I discovered this the first night by falling out of my narrow bed. My other hardship was the battle of the mosquitos. I must have tasted sweet, they all seemed to want a bite. My body reacted badly to them, and each bite raised a swollen red welt around it. One day when we were bored, I got Anna, to count them—216 bites on my tiny body. On bad mosquito days, the nights were worse—the itching troubled my sleep. I must have gotten used to the mosquitoes, though. Most of my memories of the jungle are idyllic.

The rules in our new home were minimal. I was told strictly to keep out of the banana grove in the front yard. Snakes made their home there. I was also told to keep my eyes open for certain spiders, and to ***never ever*** put my hand into a container of any kind without looking first. The first example of this was the tins in the shed which held nails and screws—we should never grab for something without checking first. I was not necessarily the most obedient child, but I was never tempted to break those two rules!

My mom had found a puppy just before we moved, and when she brought it home my dad questioned what she would do with it when we moved. The puppy was a tiny thing, which she named Pip Squeak because he was so little and he squeaked continuously—until he learned to bark. She informed my dad that we would be glad for a pet in the jungle and Pip Squeak would be coming along in the DC-3. He grew rapidly in his new jungle yard, so we called him Pip. He traded his squeaking for barking, which on occasion alerted us that the snakes had left their grove.

My mom was vocal about her main complaint. She got sick of the food rather quickly and joked that the only way to change the menu was to change the order you ate your food. "If we don't want rice, meat, and bananas, we can just have meat, rice, and bananas." The bananas were plantain, fried to a slimy, mushy mass. Not my favourite!

As a treat we sometimes had chicken for a meal or two. Chickens came in payment for flying services, and we kept them in our backyard orange grove. Mom wanted eggs, but when she gave up that dream we had a special chicken dinner for consolation. When she decided it was the day for chicken, my dad had to chase one around in the orange grove and then chop its head off, not a job he enjoyed. From my perch behind the big kitchen window I learned first hand what "running around like a chicken with his head cut off" actually looks like. The chicken and my dad made quite a pair, with my mom out there cheering Dad on.

My mom seemed content, except for the menu, to live in this remote village, with a slow, jungle pace of life. She enjoyed visiting women and hearing their stories even if they were remarkably similar. Most woman in our village had given birth to twelve children, but only two were still living.

Mom did our laundry by hand, and wondered why the missionary who lived there before us had employed someone but then complained bitterly that the house helper stole things. If you can do it yourself, then do it yourself. That was mom's way. My part of helping with laundry was to get a small quota of buckets of water up out of the well. My sister did more because she was nearly two years older than me, not quite eight.

While we lived here, my dad built himself a ham radio in his spare time. He spent most evenings working on it with Anna beside him, eagerly helping. She would study the plans and then scour the box of parts for the tiny "servos" he would need next. I itched to help, but was told I was too little. I stood by watching, feeling a little resentful and redundant. With this new radio Dad was able to keep in contact with his family in New Zealand and friends from the church in Toronto where he had met

Mom. Phones and electricity were not part of jungle life. This was our connection to other villages, the big city, and the rest of the world. Dad was way ahead of his time.

We only lived in the jungle for one year, but it felt like home to me. We settled in quickly, and occasionally Anna or I would be allowed to go along on my dad's flights. We visited a couple living in a much bigger town where there were motorcycles for taxis and a shop with ice cream for sale. We spent a few days with a couple of women who travelled up and down the river on a boat. One day we went across the river and visited the Brazilian town on the other side. They had electricity and cars in Brazil.

On our Christmas holiday from school we spent a week at the lepers' colony where my dad was the administrator. Two sisters, women in their sixties, staffed the leprosarium on Lake Victoria—I wondered who named the lake that? The sisters had been there for years, living together in a simple but cozy house on the far end of the landing strip. They had furniture and real living room chairs and had clearly created a home.

The other end of the airstrip ran to the lake, where we would swim each afternoon, saving us the need of a shower. This was handy, since there was no shower. We stayed in a wooden guesthouse beside the runway; it was up on stilts in case the lake flooded. There was no furniture inside except for the beds. I begged to walk around to all the huts and visit the lepers of this secluded colony.

My dad gave me a walking stick about three feet long and told me to use it to measure the distance between myself and the people that I visited. This was another rule I had no temptation to break. The people with leprosy had missing limbs or fingers, usually bandaged, but I felt the threat of their horrible disease. However, they were friendly and seemed to appreciate these chatty visits with "Elenita," conversations like those I had enjoyed with the staff in the boarding school. Each day I made my way around to greet them, stopping at each hut for a conversation. One day they told me about a snake that came out of the lake and ate their duck, whole. They killed the snake and retrieved the duck for their supper. I didn't believe them, but when I checked with the sister-nurses, they said it was true.

When the school break ended in August we all flew to the big city, Cochabamba, where we had lived before moving. The mission school was located about ten kilometres out of town. My parents had spent the previous two years living at the boarding school where my mom was in charge of the dorms and the kitchen. My dad had been the principal and the classroom teacher for grades 5-8.

We went back a little early as I had to get a tonsillectomy, and my mom stayed for a few extra days while I recuperated. I then joined the grade one class, a few days late. My throat was still sore, but I could eat, so it was time to move forward. Mom left me in the girl's dorm with a stranger as my roommate. Anna shared a room with some girls from her grade three class. Later in the year we were allowed to share a room for a few weeks.

My mom's best friend, Milly (Aunt Milly to us) was my dorm mother. She had two rooms at the end of the hallway where we would go for devotions before we went to bed at night. If I couldn't sleep, I would go to see Milly and climb into bed with her. She didn't mind, but I knew if I did this too often the other girls would resent my special treatment. If a teacher treated me too nicely, I also got heckled for that.

The school was familiar to me, and I knew all the kitchen helpers, but I didn't have the same freedom I had enjoyed the year before when I spent my spare time with them in the kitchen. I didn't hate being in boarding school, it was part of a normal world to me, but that year I mostly felt "lost". I had learned to play independently, but I loved family times of being together. At boarding school, most of the time I felt very alone, especially at the end of the school day. Only about half the kids lived in dorms, and the other half went home each afternoon, on a special school "*rapido*"—a large van that served as public transport the rest of the day.

On weekends, some of the dorm kids were allowed to go home with the day kids if we were invited. There were strict rules doling out these occasional visits. Mom's list of what I would need for a weekend was taped to the inside of my suitcase. I would carefully pack three pairs of socks, underwear, pyjamas, and clothing, on Thursday night, so that on Friday I could quickly grab my case and ride the *rapido* home with a friend. I felt very uncertain of myself, staying in the home of complete strangers, since I didn't know the parents, but I loved not having to spend the long weekend hours alone at the school.

A few days after my sixth birthday in October, which had passed by almost unnoticed, a parcel arrived from my mom. It had something she had made for me, maybe a dress and also a home-baked cake. She had made two cakes, one for me and one for Anna. Mine was coloured pink, because I loved all things pink. It was baked in a cleaned out tuna can, so it was the perfect size for me. I felt very loved and special that she had remembered and sent my own cake, in the colour I loved.

I would have much preferred to stay at home with my parents for that year. It seems in retrospect that it would have been quite feasible for my dad, a primary school teacher-cum-pilot to have kept me on the "straight and narrow" as my mom liked to say.

But that was not the way things were done in those days. The older missionaries, including the two leper-nursing sisters, were openly critical that my parents had brought us along to Bolivia at all. They should have left Anna and me with relatives in either New Zealand or Canada, to be brought up there.

Perhaps that year influenced my parents more than I realized, however. A few years later when my dad returned to his role as school principal, he envisioned a scheme for families from remote towns to come to the school for six weeks of each semester, then return home with their books. He then flew a traveling teacher from town to town to spend a week with each family. Thus he combined his teaching career, his piloting job, and his visionary gifts to good advantage.

When I look back, it seems we spent more than just one year in the house in the jungle. I was happy there, with neighbours to visit and Pip to play with. But before I started grade two, my dad figured out a way to continue his flying services for the jungle missionaries and the leprosarium while living in the big city. By changing the home base of the aircraft, he expanded the circuit of flying services to missionaries in equally isolated mountain locations. This move back to Cochabamba allowed us to commute to school with the day students. I could now invite my former roommates home for the weekends, to my delight.

We moved back to the mission house where we had lived for our first year in Bolivia. This time we had an apartment upstairs, and my mom was the manager of guest services. She changed the weekly menu plan, boldly implementing a new, less predictable menu with greater variety. This caused a few ruffled feathers for the older missionaries who were permanent residents, but she stuck by her decision.

Mom also decided to upgrade the big room where most mission meetings were held. Everyone living in town came to the Monday night prayer meeting, and some rousing hymns were sung in this room, especially on the nights when my dad played the piano. He could pound out jubilant and extraordinary arrangements of any hymn. His creativity livened up the singing considerably.

Each Monday night I lay in bed listening to the mission community singing favourite hymns. I loved "And Can it Be", which invited the most inspired piano playing and enthusiastic singing. I appreciated hymns that were sung with gusto.

When my mom went out to order the linoleum for this large space, there were only two options: dull grey or vivid red with a robust motif of flowers around the edge. She opted for the brilliant red, to match the flourishes of my dad's piano skills. She said, "I'd love to be a fly on the wall when Brother Joe sees *this* on the floor." I could tell by her tone of voice that she expected a reactionary response from "Brother Joe", the current mission director. With the fresh red linoleum this room looked more like a ballroom than a space for a prayer meeting.

There were few things that threatened the safety of my world in these early years. One night my sister played with the settings on the beach-style folding chair that I was sitting in. The chair crushed my fingers when it collapsed. My mom refused to come to my aid, saying I was just being dramatic in my screaming. One fingernail was dangling by a few threads of skin, so I felt justified.

Our *rapido* got into a crash on the way to school one morning, and I got a three centimetre gash in my forehead. The other kids went on to school, but I was taken home by a teacher wearing a blouse covered in my blood. When my mom saw her, she was afraid the news was going to be much worse than it was. She was quite as dramatic in her relief as I had been in the loss of my fingernail. We went to the clinic run by her versatile gynecologist, Dr. Kovacs, and he stitched my split forehead.

Every Friday night was a game night at our house open to all. On Saturdays my parents would find exciting places to visit, new roads to explore, and picnic spots to enjoy. This was a tradition they had started as dorm parents at the boarding school. Most of the excursions we made included intrigued newcomers who loved to join in my dad's search for adventure. We would often look for unmapped roads my dad had spotted from the air. We did not live a dull or uninspired life. It seemed like every year brought something new, and I loved the variety, all the chances to explore.

Change was the landscape of our lives; stability came from navigating the transitions as a family, together.

⁜ The Weeping Trees ⁜

. . . . .

⁜ March 2015 ~ Ellen ⁜

I moved to North Africa over 18 years ago when my children were small. Having lived here this long, it is now as much my home as any place has been. Memories of Bolivia, especially my earliest years, hold a special place in my heart. Sometimes my surroundings here in North Africa bring back glimpses of those earlier times.

The weather is nearly perfect today, a spring day in 2015. It brings me back to a feeling of the familiar—bougainvillea in bloom, birds singing, wind rustling through eucalyptus trees. When I scuttle back to my memories of the city I grew up in, there are many days of perfect weather. My mom used to comment often on how fortunate we were to live in such a moderate climate, no real winter or summer, just 80 degrees Fahrenheit all year around.

On Thursday afternoons I pray with a group of women here; we have become close friends, companions on our spiritual journey. We begin our time by sharing anything God has been showing us in the past week. On this day, one friend brings Psalm 46. We start with the first words, "God is our refuge and strength," and pray through parts of this psalm. The powerful words stir my soul toward trust.

Psalm 46 is never a "new" passage to me. It always evokes old memories. It is tied strongly to the distant past. In the echo of the words of the first three verses, I can instantly be back in my mom's room in a private clinic in Bolivia, over 40 years ago.

I wonder what fears my mom was fighting as she entered that clinic. She had endured a stillbirth in this clinic—did that memory chase her through the hallways? Did she ponder the possibility that this might be the pathway toward death? The words of Psalm 46 take me back to this complex mix of comfort and discomfort at the brokenness of life itself.

As we read Psalm 46, I am back in time:

It is the night before Mom's surgery in June 1973, and we read this passage together as a family. But that is not the beginning of her slipping toward the valley of death. The story begins on an ordinary, yet very unusual evening, at the beginning of that year.

January 1973 ~ Elenita

We are invited to the Redykes' home for supper on a balmy summer evening—it is a familiar place; we have been here many times before. We walk past the moonflower tree on our way through their gate. I love leaving the Redykes' house at night. In the dark, the moonflower has a sweet, strong scent. By day it is a drooping white lily-shaped flower on a small tree. By night it is sheer paradise, with a fragrance few night flowers can match.

This evening holds events that no one expects. It marks the beginning of the end of my mom's life, but none of us knows that—not until much later. Mrs. Redyke is a great Southern cook and entertainer, but for me the best part of going there is her iced tea. She gave me the recipe when I asked—an oral explanation of course. Mine never turns out like hers, which lives as a legend in my memory.

During supper, while I am savouring each sip of the sweet tea, my mom suddenly jumps up and makes a dash for the bathroom. Everything about this sudden activity is unusual, not a bit like her. It is abrupt, frantic, alarmed. And alarming. I am unnerved by this.

Her apologetic reappearance at the table does nothing to reassure me. My mom offers an effusive and elaborate apology, overly elaborate. Perhaps she also feels unnerved. Mrs. Redyke tries to reassure her but the rest of the evening feels uncertain to me.

I am glad when we leave and I can walk past the familiar moonflower, the scent of it settling my fears. If ever an aroma could sing, this one does, and the serenade is good for my troubled heart. I just turned 11 three months earlier, and these unsettling fears, though not common, are an emerging part of my awareness. I am no longer the carefree child of even a year ago.

In the following weeks, I don't notice any further symptoms that mark my mom's illness. I ask her about this night and get the answer that it must have been a passing problem, unexplained, but now gone. I am glad to hear this, though perhaps there are problems and she does not tell me.

In April, a flu virus hits hard, and various community members are violently ill. When it comes to our house, it misses the rest of our family, but my mom is ill with alarming severity. Her fever soars, she scarcely leaves her bed, and her good friend Milly comes over to care for her. I tiptoe past her room, knowing I should not disturb any troubled sleep she might be finding.

I spend the weekend in my room, praying that God will spare her. I am petrified my mom is in imminent danger of losing her life. Every time I stop to consider this, I beg God to leave her with us. The idea of a life without her produces an alarm in me that tastes as tangible and as terrible as charcoal in my mouth. I am afraid to think about what that life would be like. Compelled by apprehension, I pray with panicky words, pleading with God.

God spares her life, and I am deeply grateful. The relief is a sweet, sweet moment. My prayers are answered. God is on my side.

As we come to the end of the school year, life resumes its familiar rhythm. There is a recital to prepare for. There is the annual excitement of my mom's sewing extravaganza. Mom has the ability to create patterns for anything and loves to watch the fashions in Canada and sew stylish clothing for Anna and me to wear. She once made a bridal gown without a single slip of tissue paper for the pattern; she is rightfully proud of her genius for sewing.

My mom doesn't let us down—she has, in fact, planned and brought back from Canada a length of white polyester which she uses to create matching sailor suits with wide boat collars trimmed in navy blue. I do not enjoy the slippery feeling of this fabric on my skin, but I don't tell my mom about that. I enjoy the special collar and the embossed gold buttons that trim it with feminine style. The photo that I recall for many years to come when I want to see her face is taken the day these suits are finished and we try them on for the first time. Her face is lit by a beaming smile, full of triumph over her accomplishment.

This is the last memory I have of Mom being energetic in this way. Her lively personality slowly becomes more and more subdued as the life in her ebbs away.

If the beginning of her illness was the dinner at Redykes', the beginning of the end of my mom's life comes with the surgery scheduled for the first week of our school holiday. I arrive home from school one day in May to find her in our yard talking to a friend with tears slipping down her cheeks as they converse. What I hear alarms me, and I wait to ask her about the conversation when we are alone.

She has a tumour, she tells me. Dr. Kovacs says it is benign, so that means she isn't truly sick, and the surgery won't be for several more weeks. But she dislikes this outcome quite intensely. Mom explains that she has had several surgeries in her life, and she does not want another one—this is why she is crying. It is a new experience for me, finding my mom fragile in health and in her emotions and not knowing what I can do to help. She tries to reassure me, telling me everything will be fine. I begin to feel the need to take care of her.

On the evening before Mom is due to have the surgery, we plan to drop her off at Dr. Kovacs' clinic. I ask her what we will all do, again fretting my way through these unfamiliar, uncharted paths. We will have supper, just like a normal day. She won't eat with us, but the rest of the family will eat and then we'll all take her to the clinic. My sister and I are welcome to come along; this is what has caused my distress—that she will leave without me. It is a sober procession that evening.

The clinic is a converted "mansion" in an older part of the city, dating back to a more colonial era. The grandeur of the front entry gives a feeling of stability. And the elegant, weeping branches of the mature trees in this neighbourhood sweep away my fears, quelling the anxiety that hovered over me during supper. We enter through the familiar front doors and wait in the stately front hallway reception area with a grand staircase circling to the second floor.

I have been to visit several women who gave birth here, delivering flowers and baby gifts with my mom. My head was stitched up in the surgical room after the rapido accident when I was eight. It turned out fine. Mom's finger was sewn back on by this competent gynecologist, Dr. Kovacs, who served as a surgeon in WWII. She cut it off cleanly in a commercial meat grinder, brought it with her to the clinic, and he stitched it back on saying, "We may as well try. I've seen stranger things happen." And it worked, though she never regained feeling in that fingertip. I have confidence in her doctor.

Mom's room is on the second floor, and we all traipse up, carrying her belongings. It is a lovely room; I've been in it before, but I can see that my mom is clearly unsettled. She worries about the reality that the clinic has no elevator, so the staff will have to carry her up these stairs on a stretcher after the surgery. She will still be unconscious, so I wonder why this troubles her. Perhaps it is just a place for her to expend her own anxiety.

My dad asks if we can read a scripture together, and then pauses. "Is there something one of you would like to read?" —he has not thought of what to read. I am eager to offer what pops into my mind: Psalm 46. We have studied this in our Bible class; I remember the first line, and it seemed like an appropriate promise to read.

God is our refuge and strength, a helper
who is always found in times of trouble.
Therefore we will not be afraid, though the
earth trembles and the mountains topple
into the depths of the seas,
Though its waters roar and foam and the
mountains quake with its turmoil. CSB

The two verses after the initial promise alarm me. I have forgotten that this psalm describes the mountains disappearing into the sea. It occurs to me that something bad might happen, and I feel the familiar panic from the April flu fight pushing toward me. I reassure myself with what I learned in April. God is going to answer prayer, and Mom will be fine. I shove the anxieties to the back of my mind, into a box, and shut the lid. I will sit on the lid if necessary, to keep from tasting that horrible fear again. I have successfully quelled my fears—so successfully that the rest of the school holidays pass with the lid safely on that box.

The surgery goes well, and Mom starts to recuperate. Each day follows a pattern, as she spends the next week recovering in the quiet leafy neighbourhood, with a room that overlooks the clinic's garden. I leave home each day after lunch and do some grocery shopping in a familiar small shop because there are no large supermarkets. From there I walk to the clinic to visit for the afternoon.

It takes nearly an hour and a half for me to get to the clinic, with the shops about halfway in the journey. I bring my bag of goods to show my mom, and she admires my growing expertise. I have often gone with her on shopping outings. Doing this alone gives me a sense of achievement.

I daily water the plants she has been given. My favourite one is the delicate cyclamen which I have never seen before. It has to be watered from the dish below. It has translucent petals in a combination of blushing pink and deep magenta that I love.

We play a game or read together, something quiet and easy, as she is still in some pain and very tired. I long to go down to the garden I can see below us, but she is too weak for that. Later in the afternoon my dad comes, bringing Anna with him, and we all go home together.

When Mom comes home, our routine continues, now in the quiet of our own home. I am not sure that many in our community realize she is not recovering fully from the surgery. The doctor did not find the benign tumour he had diagnosed as the cause of her illness. He has told her the pain was from adhesions, thick scars, from earlier surgeries. He did some repairs, and I suppose he says, like with the cut-off finger—"we will see what happens."

I carry on doing the shopping now in the mornings. Sometimes I work on a sewing project Mom has inspired in me. She bought me a doll with normal proportions, about three times the size of a Barbie doll, so I can learn to design patterns and sew. If I start out with simple things, she says I can do this well. Whenever I make something new and show her, she gives me feedback—encouragement with insights on how to do better. I enjoy sharing these projects with her.

We spend many afternoons playing Scrabble when her energy has been renewed by a short nap after lunch. My mom can play Scrabble while lying on the couch, which seems to be her new place of refuge. Other games wear her out, but Scrabble can go on for hours, and I have hours to spend by her side. In her youth she won prizes in Scrabble tournaments, so we play this even though it is not my favourite. Playing this game is a gift I hope will make her feel strong again. I get better at Scrabble as my vacation goes along, but I don't learn to love it.

In August, before school starts, we have planned a week away at the home of some friends in a part of Bolivia we have never visited together. My dad has flown there several times and wants to take us there. It is a region famous for fossils, and Anna's interest in this fuels the plan. Fossils sound rather uninteresting to me.

The night before we leave, my dad announces that my mom will be staying in the mission house, which was our home at one time. It is a familiar place to all of us, and she will rest better there. The trip would be too tiring for her.

I try to protest. It is far from acceptable to me to leave her behind. I am told the decision has been discussed and made, and my protests are quickly silenced.

I miss her constantly throughout the week, but it doesn't occur to me that this is my future—a whole life ahead of me without her.

I regret that decision to leave her behind. It is not mine to regret, but I still have a sorrow that we didn't make the effort to fill that last week with a good family memory. Other family holidays contain memories of my mom walking along singing old tunes, teaching me the words, and conversing about the meanings. This holiday feels quiet and empty without her company.

When the three of us come home we eagerly return to the guesthouse to find my mom. The reunion feels awkward; I am uneasy. We find her standing with someone who is asking her about her health and commenting on her weight loss. She is joking about how she has finally lost all the weight she tried to get rid of for years and shows us how she pinned her woollen skirt with giant safety pins to keep it from sliding off her hips. It's a skirt she hasn't worn for a few years because it was too small before she got ill.

The weight loss has been slow enough that I failed to notice. In this moment she seems fragile, both physically and emotionally, despite her good humour. I am afraid to hug her, afraid to hurt her.

We return to our own house, and school starts within a few days. The flurry of a new teacher and a new year absorbs my attention.

And somehow we have arrived at the end of my mom's life, without noticing the signposts that marked this valley of shadows. One day, a week into the new school year, I come home to discover my parents packing. My dad announces that Dr. Kovacs has advised them to go to Canada for medical help, the sooner the better. By a miracle, he has found tickets that leave the next day. Cheerfully he reminds Anna and me that his brother and his wife are coming. They will arrive less than 48 hours after my parents' departure, so we will have lots to do, showing them around our town.

The flickering fear I had when we read Psalm 46 is about to become reality. The mountains are, in fact, about to be swallowed into the seas, but I do not see it coming. And I am not ready.

⁂ Wind in the Curtains ⁂

. . . . .

⁂ March 2015 ~ Ellen ⁂

I have a daughter who is growing into adulthood. She knows the craggy landscape of life's cruelty. She has experienced more deep personal loss in her short lifetime than many adults. Today she tells me of the worst day of her life. She asks about mine, and I describe how I felt the day after my mom died. As we talk, my daughter wants to know more. It seems like the right day to tell her.

It was not just one day that was the worst day of my life—there are three of them, a trio of worst days all connected. They are wound together like a cord, a strong and terrible cord, marking my life into two chapters.

My mom died on a Tuesday. I was not at school. For the past week I had gone to school where we prayed every day as a class that my mom would get well. I was inside a sphere of blind faith. We prayed and I thought God would answer. It did not occur to me that she might die. I had been frightened by the chance of death a few months before, when she was desperately sick with flu. But in this last week of her life, the obvious eluded me. I was surviving in a world of oblivion. I don't know if others were closer to knowing the truth. I don't know if that matters.

The doctor had somehow failed to diagnose Mom's cancer. She had been sick and growing slowly worse over the past six months. I can remember the day it started, but no one realized that she was in her last weeks when she flew to Canada from Bolivia. Somehow hope in the medical magic of a Canadian hospital fended off all thoughts of death.

August 29, 1973 ~ Elenita

It has been ten days since my parents left for Canada. I beg to stay home from school. Maybe I can't contend with the stresses of the situation, but I have a cold, so it is my excuse to stay in bed. My dad's brother is at our house with his wife. They have arrived for a visit to Bolivia on their world tour and are taking care of Anna and me.

As an uncle and aunt, they are better than other relatives I've met. They are schoolteachers and enjoy being around children. They are used to keeping life in order with the predictability of routine and regulations. They confidently make decisions, and if you stay inside the boundaries, everything is fine—life runs smoothly. Intuitively, I sense this about them. If I agree to what they want, everything will be okay. I have been brought up with a strong value of compliance—it is not my place to rock the boat.

On this Tuesday I have stayed in my bed, reading, sometimes pretending to be asleep when they come to check on me. I don't enjoy chatting with them. My uncle and aunt leave the house shortly after lunch, going across town to where another foreigner has a ham radio, so they can talk to my dad and get the news. They do this each day, and they tell us we will be able to talk to him next Sunday, about two weeks after my parents' departure.

On this day, when my uncle and aunt come home, there is a quiet sober air about them, and I sense the boundary is clear, though unspoken. "Don't ask." This does not alarm me, I am old enough to get the vibes on silence, but not old enough to sense the darkness of the news.

They disappear and leave me alone, waiting for Anna to come home from school. She is later than usual. There is a storm building, but I am cloudy in my head and not aware of the lightning that is about to hit my soul.

Finally Anna arrives, and the three of them come sit in my room, on the two parallel beds. The one beside me used to be Anna's, neatly made with the pink and white seersucker bedspread Mom made for our beds in the jungle. My uncle straightforwardly relays the facts with a harshness embedded in the simplicity of the news. He is sorry, but my mother's life is over. She has gone to be with the Lord. I sense they may want to hug me, but I don't know them well enough to want their touch.

One of them decides to pray. I don't want to pray —I think that is a bad idea. I don't want God's touch either. I don't know what I want, but this is not it. I want my mother, that's what I want—she would know what to say, how to comfort me. I start to realize that I am never going to see her again, and the horror of that realization is like a bomb that blows all my limbs off but leaves me alive and aware of all the pain and devastation it has caused.

I look at the window, and the sun is shining. The breeze is dancing through the curtains, making them look jolly, cheerful. The world is acting as if nothing has changed, which is completely wrong. The sun's warmth doesn't match my newly-transformed inner world, where everything is black and vacant, and I realize there are two realities. I am caught in a huge chasm, a vacuum between them.

My uncle prays, but I can't hear his words, I don't want any of this to be real. I want these two strangers to go away. But first I need to know, I want to know: Why?

They relate the stark facts and for the first time I hear the dreaded word, cancer. My mom was diagnosed with cancer three days ago. No one expected she would die this quickly. She fell asleep in the evening and went into a coma at 3:00 a.m. The nurses called my dad to come, but by the time he arrived she had died. She died alone.

My uncle and aunt leave my room, I don't remember what happens next, but falling asleep feels wrong. Sleeping would end this pain. I would like to fall asleep because I might even wake up and find this day was a dream. I hope it is a dream. But falling asleep would be wrong.

It is a blur, the rest of this day. I don't think anyone comes to visit or to say anything else to me, but my sister has an encounter that she regrets for years to come and doesn't share with me until forty years have passed. I am glad for the absence of such a memory in my file of this day's events.

The next day has clear and vivid moments between foggy ones. My aunt and uncle take us to a lake, a quiet place that our family has been to a few times on a picnic. It is a familiar, outdoor setting, and I sit alone on a grassy knoll overlooking the lake. Perhaps I spend the whole day sitting there, I don't know. I don't talk to anyone, I don't want to be with anyone, but as I look out at the lake, I start to take in the meaning of this loss. I think about all the things my mom is going to miss, all the times I will be without her in my life. It is overwhelming.

Today my limbs feel completely intact, my arms and legs are useful and keep me away from the strangers and my sister. But my torso feels like it is not intact. Today the bomb has gone off in my heart, and I physically look down at my chest to make sure it isn't gaping open with my innards hanging out. It is hard to believe that everything is exactly as it always is and has been—my chest is in one piece, my heart must still be beating inside. I feel as though there is a cavernous hole in me, and my life has drained away—gushed out of me in a giant flood of grief.

I remember a story of a woman who survives a stabbing. She looks down at herself and sees her own intestines oozing out of the slash wound across her stomach. I expect to see something like that when I look down at where my heart is located. I look fine, but that is a shock—I am actually not intact, not healthy and whole.

I think that I probably will not survive this grief.

I think that all I want is my mom to come and comfort me. She and I know how to talk about these things.

I realize I will never see her again.

And that makes my hole even bigger, a growing void where my soul should be—has always been. My mind goes blank and I stare at the lake. I could just stop breathing, just like that, just stop. And maybe I will be gone, dead and gone, too. And that seems like a good solution.

I don't know how long I sit there with these thoughts, it seems like it might be all day.

I tell my daughter this story because she shared her grief and asked me about mine—and it was time to tell her.

And I tell her because I can. Until now, I was not able to talk my way through some parts of this story. Another memory comes to me, so I share it as well. I can't remember what day this happened, but the images, the feelings, and the thoughts, are crystal clear.

It is a day, shortly after I return to school, after my mom's memorial service, when I take up the "normal" routine of life again. Life will not feel normal to me for a long time to come, but I return to the routine of school life because there is no alternative.

I can't remember the order of all the events of the next few weeks, but I can remember my first day back to school. Hardly anyone has anything to say to me. They all feel terribly awkward and unsure of how to treat me, but I feel their eyes watching me—questioning if I am okay. One kid says, "I'm really sorry about your mom," but it is awkward, and it feels like everyone else watching is afraid to come near me. Maybe it is my fear of having them come near; I feel as though I might break into pieces. My heart is fragile, like a soap bubble—if someone touches the pain, the bubble might break. It is better to be soul-less.

My teacher tells me that if I need to leave class at any time, I can do that. So one day I leave. I cannot think about my work, so I excuse myself to go to the bathroom, only I don't come back to my class.

I go to a room in the old empty dorms, no longer used during the school year. I sit on a bed in this silent familiar room. Maybe when I was six, this was my bedroom for a while. In my year in the dorm, we moved from room to room every month, so there is a familiar feeling here. In this quiet spot, I start to cry.

A girl named Carol walks by and decides to come in. She is from my sister's grade, so I doubt there is any reason she is here. I doubt someone sent her to find me. But who knows? Carol and her brother are adopted. Her brother is in my class, and he is always in trouble. Kids talk about how they have no real parents, though I think their adoptive parents would be horrified by this.

Carol does not seem comfortable with warmth and compassion and hugging. If she was, I think she might have held me in her arms, and this moment might have gone quite differently. But I am alone in the room, crying just enough for her to notice. She comes in and sits beside me on the saggy old dorm bed. She asks a few questions, and I try to answer them, but as I do so, I start to sob, almost wail, and I double over in the pain of this moment of trying to share my grief with another person. As she becomes more awkward, her nervousness attracts my attention.

I realize that Carol is getting upset, that she is probably blaming herself, and that she is scared. I cannot stop the sobbing, but I too become afraid. I am afraid that I will lose my self, my very being, in the great chasm of grief that is within me. There is nothing else that is me in this moment. I am not Ellen the girl who wins the push-up contest every year, or Ellen the girl that doesn't play the piano like everyone else but plays the flute, or Ellen the girl that always gets all the spelling words right. I am just Ellen, the girl with nothing but a hole for a soul. I have become the void.

And I am scared. I am scared that I will never be more than this hole.

I am scared that I will forget how to live.

I am scared I will remember how to live and forget my mother.

I am just scared. And alone. Too scared and alone to entertain these emotions I have nearly drowned in with Carol sitting beside me, watching nervously, not touching me.

So I stop myself, I stop my grief, and I bury the terrible emotion of these moments in a dark, and even deeper hole inside of me. The alarm caused by the primal pain, the unfiltered agony of this loss, is like the fear of Pandora's Box. If I let the lid come off, and the pain gets out, it will consume my world with me in it, and I will never get it all back into the box again. So I close the lid tightly as I stifle the sobbing and wipe away my tears. I refuse to come back to this searing pain, not even in my memory—until ten years have passed. I live with the dull ache, the pain that comes with keeping the lid on—the constant effort of corralling the unspeakable. This throbbing ache consumes my energy but doesn't threaten my existence.

And that is how I survive.

⁂ Red Linoleum ⁂

▪ ▪ ▪ ▪ ▪

⁂ August 2009 ~ Ellen ⁂

It is August 2009, a warm month in Northern Thailand, the weather matching the friendly culture of this country. The beautiful flowers, the sticky humidity, the tropical fruit, the slow pace of life—all bring back a sense of "home," a sliver of my childhood in Bolivia. There is a familiar joy in the warm rain that falls on us on our first day here—warm raindrops found only in jungle climates.

With my family, I am attending a conference in Thailand. Another attendee is a familiar face from my Bolivian childhood. His face reminds me more of his dad than of the boy who grew up in Anna's class in elementary and middle school. But this is another slice of the past, and when he finds me at lunch on the final day, he offers a priceless gift.

Another "boy," David, also from Anna's class, will be stopping by to pick him up later that afternoon. David is traveling with his mom—and perhaps if I come to the foyer, we can all meet together for a few minutes. I eagerly ask for the meeting time and get a vague answer—there is no set time. That little piece of Bolivia is still living inside all of us—it will just be sometime in the late afternoon. Since I am committed to being in a final seminar, I ask him to come to get me so I won't miss this encounter.

This reconnection, a scant fifteen minutes of my day, is much more than it seems on the surface. The woman is not just a schoolmate's mother—she is the woman that sang at my mom's memorial service. I had no personal relationship with her, though we called her "Aunt Betty," in missionary tradition. The gift of her song, on the day set aside to bid my mother farewell, was the one part of the service that reached me with a flicker of hope in the midst of the loss.

I remember moments of the day of my mom's death and the following day with crystal clarity. But the following three days are a fog, a blur with nothing to distinguish them from each other. And then the day of my mom's memorial service arrives, and fragments of memories, like shards in a kaleidoscope, slide together and create a pattern to my recollection of that day.

September 31, 1973 ~ Elenita

I get up on the day of my mom's memorial service and get dressed in a haze. My dad has not returned from Canada, so it feels strange and hollow to go to a service for my mom without him. Less than a week has passed since the day she died—I have not yet returned to school. That will be tomorrow's task. I should be glad for today's numbness which makes it possible for me to show up at the door of the meeting room in the mission house where the service is held.

This big room is next to our old apartment; it feels almost like home. My old bedroom was behind big double doors at the far end, opposite the entrance.

Monday night prayer meetings started with the surging of voices singing hymns of faith—harmonies of hope, grace, and truth. If there is a phrase hanging over today's service, it comes from my favourite hymn. "Bold I approach the eternal throne, And claim the crown, through Christ my own." This is my mom's day to approach that throne, but I cannot hear this—my senses are dulled by how tired the grief has made me.

The back double doors are open for the memorial service, and there are chairs set up in my empty bedroom—there will be a crowd of people, probably the biggest crowd I've ever seen in here. I glance up, see faces, and feel overwhelmed by so many people looking at me. I fix my eyes on the floor as I enter.

The red linoleum glares back up at me, daring me to remember the day it was delivered and installed. My mom's delight in replacing worn-thin, drab beige flooring with vibrant red linoleum is all through this giant room. The memory of her happiness taunts me.

I want to remember my mom this way—a person bubbling with fun, anticipating the ripple effect of her choice, all the way up to the mission director. Each happy memory I have of her delivers an equally sharp stabbing pain of loss, cutting off the joy with this thought: I will never again hear her laughing, joking voice. I walk to my seat in the front row, thinking these thoughts, but my aching heart is numb. I hear her voice in my head, "I'd love to be a fly on the wall when Brother Joe sees this." The red linoleum is her laughter. I glare back down at the floor. Perhaps this staring contest will lock out the pain, hold back the tears.

This room is about joy, not mourning and sorrow. I don't think there has ever been a memorial service here. It feels wrong, but wrong is how my life has felt for the past five, six days. My life is wrong, it is not just a feeling. At least the screaming pain has been numbed.

Beside the podium are two huge wreaths with my mom's name on white card stock, with a black border edging them, indicating death. One of them simply says "Doña Meri," her name as she spelled it in Spanish. I know these come from the local churches where she was much loved. I'm surprised and glad that they would send their condolences in this traditional way. I notice there are more flowers, but I don't know who sent them.

I'm in the front row, sitting beside Anna, waiting, feeling unsure about how to make it through this time but not willing to miss it. The service starts with a prayer and a hymn. I cannot sing. I am upset that everyone else seems willing to sing. I'd like to stand up and scream, "Stop singing!" Singing is happy, and this is not a happy time. There must be a better way to grieve this loss than to sing hymns and pray.

The numbness in my heart spins a foggy web of timelessness around me as the service progresses. I am here, but I am not here. I am remembering as many things as I can about the last weeks of my mom's life, rehearsing her presence, in case I might forget. I fear I will forget. There are gaps in my memory—this confirms that I am forgetting, have forgotten already, will forget even more. I focus on what I can remember—what she wore, what we ate, what we did for our last weeks together.

Aunt Betty gets up to sing. She has created her own song, combining music from a hymn with words from 2 Corinthians 5, matched to the tune.

> **For we know that if our temporary, earthly dwelling is destroyed, we have a building from God, an eternal dwelling in the heavens, not made with hands. Indeed, we groan in this body, desiring to put on our dwelling from heaven since, when we are clothed, we will not be found naked. CSB**

Aunt Betty has drawn me back into the reality of the service. The words about eternity settle into my thoughts, inside the fog. My mom is in heaven, this is true—I can allow this tiny piece of the service to connect to me. Aunt Betty's music has reached me, not with comfort, exactly, but I've heard the words and felt their reality. I will write Aunt Betty's name in my Bible and come back to these verses in years to come, many times over. I will let this hope of heaven grow in me slowly.

The rest of the service is a blur. If there are words of comfort, they are not for me, but for the large crowd of friends who share the grief of my mom leaving us. She is not "mine" today; she is "ours." I wish this service was for me, for "my" mother, but it is a service full of presentations, commentary for adults: people talking and talking.

I can feel the heaviness of grief in the room. It feels vaguely like some people are here to grieve that there are two little girls left without a mother. This is a heaviness that I am not willing to share with them; it doesn't help me. These thoughts are fuzzy in my head and heart on this day, but they come clearer to me later as I look back on the service.

There is a long theological homily by Brother Joe that I am beyond hearing, then the final prayer, and the service is finally over. Relief. I make my way determinedly out the door, ahead of all the people. I am hurrying toward Milly's apartment—she lives in the apartment we lived in when I was eight, just a few steps across the foyer. It is almost like going home for me. My aunt stops me and tells me that friends who have come are expecting to greet us.

The horror of this thought is too much. I am finished with people for today. I don't know if I beg or argue but I'm sure my teacher-aunt recognizes a child whose mind is not to going to be changed. Or she avoids the scene it might make and lets me go. She stays to greet the guests with my uncle.

I sit in the office area of Milly's L-shaped bedroom. In the silence there is rest from this long dark day. Anna sits beside me; we have no words. Milly is not with us, but she appears at the door.

Milly brings a message and presses us to comply. Dr. Kovacs and his wife have come to the service. They are waiting in the foyer to greet us. He is insisting that they need to see us. Anna and I are pressured to agree to this, and the doctor and his wife come to the doorway of the apartment.

Dr. Kovacs's own grief is apparent, and his wife, also a doctor, stands beside him weeping as he speaks to us. This loss is personal to them—they loved my mom. Choking his way through the words, Dr. Kovacs expresses his sorrow at our loss but keeps on repeating, "I am sorry, I am so sorry." It feels like there is more he is not saying. What can we say to his apology? It is perplexing and upsetting. We can't say it is okay—we have nothing to offer. I want to escape from this awful conversation that offers me no comfort and demands something of me, something I haven't got.

I am not sure what he is sorry for—he did his best to cure her. He could not have saved her. I've been told there is no cure for stomach cancer. Even in Canada they could not save her.

It does not occur to me that Dr. Kovacs could have saved me from stumbling over this cliff of unknowing. Without a diagnosis of cancer, our family went on believing that all could be well. We wasted the school holiday and made no effort to say our final good-byes well. Perhaps he knows he should have seen the signs and given us the gift of facing death with dignity instead of trauma.

But I don't know this. I am confused by his emotional apology, and I notice other guests filing toward the stairs, watching us. I do not want to be this spectacle, so I escape back to the silence of Milly's study-bedroom. I cannot help the doctor with his guilt and I do not want to see more faces with layers of grief or with abnormally cheerful smiles as they glance my way.

I wait until all the guests are gone, and then we walk home in silence—my sister and I, with my uncle and aunt, the strangers who have shared these two horrible weeks of my life.

⁂ The Orange Cassette Player ⁂

. . . . .

September 1973 ~ Elenita

My dad has been away for three weeks. When he finally comes back I am aware of how unfamiliar this day is. I've been to the airport before to meet my parents. Usually the drive is filled with excitement and joy —it is different this time. I want to see him, but I am not excited. I wait, but with dread. I know when he gets off the airplane there will be a gap, another blank, another big black hole beside him—a gaping hole to match the one inside of me. This is the real black hole, the space where my mother has always been, and belongs, and should be.

And that is what happens. My dad comes out the metal doorway of the airplane and down the steps, and I am shocked at how wrong it looks. He is alone. It is one more bomb going off in my heart, a bomb that has a message attached, clearly defining my loss. The message: "This is now my life." My favourite person in the world is gone. If I let myself think about it, I will wish my dad had died instead, so I have to be careful not to let that thought unfurl in my mind. I have to be on guard, because I know in a profound way that the thought is evil, and I cannot let it become a part of me.

My dad steps out the door of the airplane wearing garishly-checkered yellowish trousers, a pin-striped shirt, and a tie that matches nothing. I hear my mom's voice saying, "I'd hate to see what he would look like if he was left to dress himself." She's right, he should carry a sign that says, "Caution: Wearer is colour-blind."

The trip to the airport, the sight of him...everything I do has the potential to bring my mom back into my thoughts. The memories pop up like the keys on a typewriter that you press and they jump. Even when I try to avoid pressing the keys, they keep popping up. The memories bring too much pain, and yet I am glad she is with me in this way.

I've already thought about how helpless my dad generally is, and I worry that he will be alone and unable to take care of himself. So here he is, on the steps of the airplane, confirming my worries.

What I don't realize is that there are much bigger things Dad is unable to handle: the grief, both his and mine. He is "old school," brought up in an era when you didn't respect people who openly showed their emotions. He is from a culture where you do not give way to grief even when it blasts through your life like a steamroller. He is stoic and strong, in a stubborn, silent way. He believes trusting God means never expressing any sadness. He greets us at the door of the terminal, and his voice sounds, if anything, deliberately cheery. He has chosen happiness.

At home we drag his bags up the long staircase to our front door. Each step takes us further into this new reality. A few hours pass. We have each fled to our familiar corners of the house, but now I venture down to my dad's office where he is sitting at his desk. He brings out a red-orange cassette player for me. It has a black leather case to protect it.

This is his gift for me, he explains. It is something he wants me to have, especially as a way to remember my mom. I guess it is to listen to tapes of her singing, which he has made over the years. What he doesn't realize is that I will not have the emotional reserve to listen to her singing for years to come—maybe never. I cannot manage her absence and enjoy her music—the two do not belong together.

I look at the cassette player with absent thoughts and little emotion, just enough emotion for tears to well up in my eyes. One or two trickle slowly down my face. This is perhaps my chance to grieve, my opening to a world of comfort that might help me start to heal. It has been three weeks since she left, and two since she died. It is a good time to be honest about the pain.

Instead my dad says to me, "Dry your tears. We have to be strong."

So that is what I do. My dad has confirmed that my decision in the sobbing moment with Carol was the best way. I swallow my wish to share my sorrows, and follow his lead—a valiant effort at cheerfulness pervades the rest of the day. At some point, my dad pulls out some mementos of our mom's last week and shares them with Anna and me. We gain some answers for where she was when she died, who came to her funeral, and why she was buried on the other side of Canada. But these details sail through my head and past my heart. None of them tell me about my mom's thoughts or feelings in her last days, and it seems like my dad might not even miss her—he seems to have disengaged himself from her warmth.

We don't mention my mom's name or talk about her again after this brief conversation. If we ever come near the subject, it is awkward and hard, like we are balancing a tall, lopsided, fragile vase on the top of a pile of misshapen books and we need to get rid of the vase before it breaks into splinters and cuts our feet to ribbons. This is how it feels to skirt the topic of the woman who was once my mother, his wife, and a kind friend to nearly everyone we know.

Our threesome family—my dad, Anna and I— manage to eat supper without much conversation each night. We fall into a nightly rhythm that saves two of us from the silence. My sister stays home doing homework after supper, and my dad and I go to visit various people for the evening, all of whom also avoid mention of my mom's name with meticulous sincerity. Except once.

On one visit, I am waiting in a hallway for my dad to finish talking to his fellow pilots. There is another guest staying in the guesthouse where they are visiting. He is Mr. Kornfield, someone I've met before, and recognize, but we have never chatted. He sits with me and we talk easily about a few things. He is generous with his time, and I sense no unease as he takes an interest in the details of my school life. When he says quietly, "I was so sorry to hear about your mom," I feel his warmth. But I say nothing. I don't know him well enough, and he doesn't ask for more. He doesn't know that he is the one person who has touched my grief with his words. He has not probed or invited my grief to his comfort, but he has reminded me that someone cares, and I will not forget this encounter.

Everyone else is silent on the topic of my mom's life. If the word "mother" or "mom" comes up, though it rarely does, I notice an awkward silence.

In all of this, it is as if a mother never existed, except in my mind. And there she is a huge wound, a badge of pain and suffering. Somehow as long as I carry this dull ache, I know I will not forget her. On days when the pain is less, or when I realize I have not thought about her for an hour or two, I feel a new fear, a fear that I will be happy again and that in my happiness I will forget who she was. Some of the memories start to fade, and I grow more fearful because this is the reality I cannot avoid.

I will forget, I know I will. And each time I forget something about her, or a time we spent together, I will lose another piece of her.

The worst thing that I can think of is that someday I will forget her altogether. I yearn with all my heart for every memory to stay crisp and clear and keep her close in that way.

But I am not in control of this. This slipping away of the crispness of my memories is a loss that controls me, not the other way around.

⁂ Those Last Words ⁂

. . . . .

I can travel back to the earliest of memories in my life and feel the softness of my mom's skin on my fingertips. She had the softest face, and I loved to touch it. This feeling is my first memory.

When I stop and recall my last moment of contact with her, there is a clarity of visual, tactile, and emotional detail that overwhelms me. In this memory, I am eleven years old. My mom, who had lost about forty pounds over the previous six months, sits in the morning sunlight on the bench seat by our front door. I stand beside her, as close as I can get, leaning carefully in case I cause her pain in her fragile state, my arm in its familiar place around her neck. My sister stands on the other side of her, not nearly as close to her as I am.

I can feel the soft fuzz of my mom's azure blue robe under my hand. I can recall, as if I just touched her five minutes ago, the softness of the skin on my mom's neck, which has given me comfort for as long as I can remember. But I have lost the look on her face, or perhaps I never took the time to notice that.

I also fail to notice my sister in this moment, though she is standing nearby.

I am overwhelmed with the emotions I feel in this memory, yet I cannot put words to them, even now. I am not fearful, and the degree of sadness is mild. I think I feel dislike—dislike for the reality I am in. I don't want to say good-bye and run down the street to catch the bus to school. It is not the intense emotion of loss in this moment that I recall perfectly. But the memory itself evokes other feelings, emotions that have come with recalling this moment, over and over, for many years.

Every time I return to this moment for the next thirty years, there is added to it the savage pain of loss—the unspeakable pain of having a loving mother one day, and a vacant hole the next. The power of this emotion, in my memory, is beyond words. The reality of this loss has not faded, not grown weaker or distant, even though decades have passed.

That blue robe will automatically become mine after she dies, and I wear it even though it is six sizes too big for me. I don't recognize I am trying to wrap myself in comfort, the comfort that is missing from those last moments with her.

This memory of our last good-bye is vividly exact in my mind, though one thing is now missing.

I can no longer remember what she said to me—not the precise words. I used to know them and even rehearse them. For years, I remembered them exactly as she said them. Not with tender value for their dearness. For years I was perplexed by why she said so little in that moment. Silence hung between us, in a long pause, as an opportunity for her to leave a legacy. A moment when she could say just a few scant words of love and affirmation, words that I would cling to for the next decades of my life.

And somehow she chose to talk about being on time for the school bus. I used to quote the words to myself, and now I can only remember the outline of the dialogue.

The card my mom mailed from the hospital gift shop in Canada presented the same problem. The card itself said nice things—in poetic, card-like language. But after all the printed, flowery phrases, she just signed it "Love, Mom," and sent it. With mail as it was, this card arrived a few days after she died. It was a funny, odd moment, opening a card from her, knowing she was gone: wanting to connect and knowing I could not. I expected and hoped it would be a message I would treasure, the precious good-bye she missed in that final moment in our hallway. That same moment, that opportunity for endearing words, hung between us once again.

Then reading it through and hoping for a personal note on the end—why did she not know to put a few words for me to cling to? She was such a smart woman, such a kind and loving mom, instinctively compassionate—why did she miss these two opportunities?

I can only guess. My guesses are rational and slightly comforting, but the longing for those words rattles in my empty insides.

❊ February 1976 ~ Elenita ❊

There is a moment, three years after my mom's death, when her words come to me through a conversation with one of her friends. We are back in Toronto, a missionary family visiting the churches that send and support us, and we stay with a family there. I have locked my wishes away in the Pandora's Box that my heart has become, and along with my sorrow, I try to keep hidden away the dislike I have for the woman my dad is now married to.

It is a lot to keep out of sight, out of reality. But who knows? I think I am fairly successful for a 14-year-old girl. I keep most of myself submerged behind a silence that is a polite façade.

The wife of the family we are staying with is driving me somewhere with just my sister. This woman, Mrs. Kay, has not had a moment alone with us until now—it's as if my stepmother fears what might be said in her absence. It seems Mrs. Kay realizes that this is her moment to convey a special message to us.

Anna sits in the back seat. I cannot see her. As we drive along, Mrs. Kay begins to tell us about visiting my mom during her last days of illness. Apparently my dad took my mom directly to the hospital when the airplane landed in Toronto, coming from Miami and before that, Lima and Bolivia. A long journey on a good day, and this had not been a good day.

So my mom came back "home" to a Canadian hospital, but maybe she was too tired to care, I don't know. No one can tell me that. Anyone who saw her during her last week of life did so by visiting her there in the hospital where she died. Mrs. Kay was one of many, I suppose, who made that pilgrimage.

She tells us that the conversation was mostly about us girls. "My girlies," my mom called us. I can hear her saying it. It is not hard to imagine her voice saying this. Mrs. Kay tells us how much my mom talked about us—how proud she was, and how we filled her thoughts in those last days.

I can't see out the window of the car, though I am staring through the pane of clear glass. My eyes are filled with tears, some begin rolling down my cheeks silently. I cannot bear to let this lady see my pain, this terrible pain that I have suppressed for three years. She is answering the longing of my heart, the wish for a note at the end of the card, and the wish for that last oft-rehearsed conversation to include words of pride, words of affirmation and of love. She is addressing one of my deepest needs, and the tears are squeezing their way out of my soul.

But I cannot let Mrs. Kay see that. If I speak, I may sob—I may even break. And if I break, I might never put myself back together again. I am Humpty Dumpty sitting on the wall, teetering toward the edge. If I fall, it might be over.

So I hang on, I stare straight ahead, and if a tear squeezes its way through my wall of self-control, I will not let it break the silence.

I don't know if Mrs. Kay is still alive, but I'd like her to know. She did the right thing. She gave me a gift that day, even if it stung like lemon in a paper cut.

Tonight, as I record this, the feeling is more of a salty ache. Tonight, alone in the midnight hours, my tears are not silent—I can cry better if I am alone and it is dark outside, and all the neighbourhood is sleeping.

Perhaps next month, or next year, I will talk and not be so alone—and that is part of why I write this.

⁂ Goodbye Pepsi ⁂

▪ ▪ ▪ ▪ ▪

In our family, pets have always been welcomed. Cats are not our favourites, but dogs have often been a part of our lives. My earliest memories of dogs include a few traumatic moments. I was chased by dogs when I was a passenger first on a bike and then later on a motorbike, in the streets of Cochabamba. And the watchdogs at the boarding school were vicious enough that if we found them off their chains, we were to get behind closed doors and call the maintenance man immediately. Despite a few close calls and a few dog bites, I still loved our pet dogs.

Pip was my first pet dog, but he grew too big to bring back from the jungle—we couldn't hide him in the DC-3, and he didn't fit in the little Cessna so he stayed with a good family in our town in the jungle.

When I was nearly ten years old, we moved into a home with a yard that allowed us to have a dog again, and Mom found someone with puppies. We became the proud owners of a miniature dachshund, and we called her Pepsi Cola. She was a rich, shiny brown colour. We all loved her cheery disposition, and laughing at her antics gave us joy. She could jump for food to a ridiculous height and would do this relentlessly—she never seemed to give up.

One day Pepsi and I were riding home together from the airport with my dad. The cab of our old Chevy truck was full, since we had other passengers along. Pepsi and I were quite happy in the truck's open back, and she stood at the edge on her hind legs, ears flapping in the wind. I had her on a leash for safekeeping, but in one second she was over the side and onto the road, and I was banging on the window to the cab. Terrified that I was about to witness her limp, dead body on the road behind us, I screamed at the top of my lungs.

My dad stopped the truck, and there was Pepsi, quivering with fear in the shadow of the tire, still alive. She had somehow survived a strange injury—the skin was all ripped off her long and already crooked tail. A quick trip to the vet solved the problem, as he lopped off her tail. The vet had already advised us to cut off her unsightly tail, but that seemed cruel—now it was a stubby little nub that waved as enthusiastically as ever, a constant reminder of the day she was saved.

Feeling responsible for Pepsi's traumatic leap from the truck, I nursed her through the pain of her amputated tail. She became my dog more than anyone else's. My favourite chore was our daily walks around the block in the morning before school and at night after supper.

In the month before my mom died, Pepsi got a funny rash on her belly and started to eat less than was usual, causing her to lose weight. Someone, my dad or the neighbour, took her to the vet, but there was no verdict on what her problem might be, so we hoped the strange rash would take care of itself.

❊ September 1973 ~ Elenita ❊

In the weeks after my mom's death, Pepsi's vague symptoms of illness persist, but my worries for her are lost in the fog of numbness and shock. Her rash and appetite deteriorate, and one day I am alarmed when I notice how bad they have become. Most days she is now lying limp and still, hardly moving. I am afraid to be afraid for her.

On the weekend before my birthday, my dad takes Pepsi to the vet for the final verdict. He comes home with her collar, wrapped in a sheet of newspaper, and he says, "I'm sorry. It was for the best."

I am left to guess that Pepsi had been deemed incurable and that her death was at the hands of the vet, who put her to sleep. I've heard of this, but I don't want to imagine what it means. I can't reach the place inside where I can be sad for the loss of this happy little dog. I wonder if her illness has any connection to my mom's death.

I have withdrawn into my silent space where all my feelings are numb—my heart has gone cold. I am only safe here if I do not feel the terrible pain of my mom's death. I certainly can't cry for my dog either, and I survive in my silo of solitude, not wanting to talk to anyone about how this feels.

But I am afraid.

Death has invaded our house yet again—death with a stealthy sense of who is vulnerable. With Pepsi's death, I spend time thinking that any one of us might be next. We just never know what is waiting. We could be here one day and gone the next. I might blink and wake up and find my dad gone, or my sister gone. I could be left all alone in the next few days or weeks.

Or I could be the next to go. Life has become precarious.

These thoughts crowd into my head and play with my fears. So I lean hard on the top of the box of darkness and try to keep all these fears from letting out the pain inside.

The next weekend my dad goes out and comes home with a new dog, a cocker spaniel. She has big, sad eyes, the opposite of Pepsi's sparkly ones. She comes from a good home with an older lady who wants to be sure that her dog is going to someone who will love her well. My dad proudly tells me that he has promised that I will be that person. But he has not even asked me if I want a new dog, a replacement for Pepsi.

Her name is Lady—she is my birthday present for the day I turn twelve. I've been trying to avoid any thoughts of my birthday—it is a day that has the potential to bring back the sting of each thought that nearly consumed me on the day after my mom died. The day I took stock of all the events I would now have to face without my mom in my life to share them. This is the first, and it is the worst, and if I could skip this birthday, I would.

I certainly do not want the gift of a dog to replace my Pepsi. We had grown to love each other through thick and thin, and I feel forlorn at her absence.

Lady becomes my daily chore, morning and night I take her out to walk on Pepsi's route. She comes sedately when I call her instead of running wildly across the tiles when she hears me taking down her leash. And she walks with dainty footsteps, nothing like the eagerness of Pepsi charging along the sidewalk. Lady brings me none of the joy I found in my first little brown dog with a stumpy tail.

⁂ Holding My Breath ⁂

. . . . . .

November 1973 ~ Elenita

If I hold my breath, can I make this pain stop, even for a minute? I think it might help, and I wish that perhaps I could hold my breath forever. I am so close to the threshold of the next world, maybe if I take one more step, I'll fall through. Perhaps that would be wonderful. It would take care of this terrible ache in my heart and perhaps absorb the darkness that threatens to swallow me.

My teacher is talking, and I am not listening. I am lost in my thoughts. I notice how strange it is to keep breathing. I don't really know what we are studying in school this year. Somehow I can learn things and remember them and write exams and yet not really know what is going on around me. Or do the teachers just give me the same grades as I got last year, and I don't have to worry about what I am learning? Maybe this is how I get passing grades.

It is Christmas time too soon, and I have to face the second thundering reminder of loss. My birthday has passed, just one day, one long day. I think I did hold my breath all day and got through it without thinking or blinking. My mom's birthday has also passed by, in November, without so much as a mention of it in our home.

But now it is Christmas time, and there is a tree and stockings and presents and holidays—and I am home all day with no one to share my thoughts, my world.

I can remember nothing from this Christmas when I look back on it. Not the tree or the stockings, though I know we get them out and go through all the stages of celebrations. I dread getting our familiar things out. I hate the pretense that all is well.

It is not.

January 1974 ~ Elenita

On New Year's Day, four months have slipped past on the calendar. We sit together to talk about this coming year, a rare conversation between my dad and his two girls. It is a conversation mapped out by my dad to tell Anna and me that he is getting married. We are amazed.

We have never met this woman my dad speaks of, though we have heard her name a few times. She has lived in Africa for twenty years and has the same career path as my parents, which is why she is the logical choice. And she never wanted children, so we are obviously the best family for her, since we are no longer children.

"You will have a new mother," my dad tells us.

It is hard to not notice how happy my dad is about this, and I don't want to spoil his joy. He really believes this web he is weaving for himself—that she will be his wife, and therefore a mother to us. That she will love him, and therefore she will love us. That we will be a family, and he won't have to worry about doing all the parenting alone, and therefore we will be complete and whole again. Life will return to a good and happy rhythm, as if nothing has ever gone wrong or been lost.

I feel one good thing: relief. I feel relieved that I no longer need to worry about how my dad will get through life without my mom. For a few months we live off my dad's hopeful expectations.

It is not well or good or fine in my heart, but we keep hearing about this new mother. How she has translated a whole Bible into a difficult language and how she is perfect for us. She cannot come to join us until June, when she finishes translating her last book of the Bible.

I am still in shock from my mom's death, and the surprise of my dad's marriage plans adds punctuation to all the sentences that express my loss. I can no longer look back, I have to look forward, and here is the answer to all my pain: I have a new mother.

Unfortunately, reality is all too predictable. I have not grieved or even had the freedom to think about my loss. It is unlikely I will do well in the next relationship.

In fact, I am honest enough with myself to admit in my inner silence that I do not want a new mother. I am still wishing for the old one to come back. Life without her would be daily torture but for the numbness that deadens some of that pain.

My dad marries on a sunny day in June. He brings his wife home from the civil ceremony on the morning of their wedding day and says, "Say hello to your new mother." He is pleased with his problem solving skills. In the afternoon there is a "church" ceremony in the same room my mom's memorial was held in. I do my best to feel happy for my dad.

Our new mother moves into our home and reinvents our family on foundations of brokenness. She is, as my dad has told us, an accomplished and amazing woman who has tackled and completed many impressive projects. This, however, is her first attempt at being a parent. She finds my cooking, dishwashing, cleaning, and laundry skills below her expectations. She announces that she will remedy that with a system of rules and punishments. I try far too hard to please her, and perhaps damage myself more than anyone in the process of discovering that I don't have the capacity to do so. I frequently find myself saying, "Maybe this report card will make her say something good." Or, "Maybe today she will like the way I fixed this..."

My unsuccessful efforts bring me to a new survival tactic. I focus my energy on corralling all my desire, wishes, and dreams that I might gain a word of praise from her into my box of broken hopes. I never get the dishes done to my stepmother's specifications. The house dust falls as fast as I clean it, so the polished furniture never gleams. Anything I make in the kitchen—a place that once brought me joy—is not as tasty as it "should" be. The first cake I make for her is a disaster and is criticized accordingly. I never make her a second.

My dad seems happy. He seems not to notice that his new wife dislikes me. I try to keep my dislike for her a secret, but the friction is wearing me down.

I have fainting spells that cannot be explained. Many weekends I find myself lying on the tile floor, sometimes remembering the slow fade of light as I collapsed there, sometimes not.

Looking back, I can only guess that perhaps my brain needed to turn off before it exploded. It chose fainting as the survival method of choice for those adolescent years.

I manage my life in this pressure cooker of silence for four years. I start planning ahead and find a way to talk my dad into letting me finish high school at a boarding school in Canada. There I will be alone and thousands of miles from a home that is no longer my home.

May 1978 ~ Elenita

I am sixteen. I'm packing up two suitcases that hold all my belongings, and moving back to Canada by myself. I am relieved to leave. I will survive more effectively with a greater distance between me and my stepmother.

The day that I leave for Canada is a few weeks before the end of the school year. My teachers have agreed to release my final grades without my finishing the year. I spend the morning at school saying goodbye to my friends, then I take the bus "home" to the house we have lived in for six years, since before my mom's death. It houses all the dark memories of her final year with us, and the years with my stepmother. I am relieved to be leaving.

My flight leaves in the early evening, about six p.m. As I walk out onto the familiar tarmac and board the waiting jet, I wonder if I will ever see this city again.

I don't look back. I don't want to. There is no "bittersweet" to this moment. It is just bitter. I wish I could leave all my unhappiness here, where it has grown inside me like a mushroom cloud. But I cannot.

That is not how it works.

⁂ My Australian Friends ⁂

. . . . . .

⁂ February 2015 ~ Ellen ⁂

Sometimes I need the dark, the silence of everyone sleeping in the house, for my thoughts to reach down beyond my surface feelings and into the raw brokenness of my soul. Forty-two years have passed since my mom died, half a lifetime. For the past two decades I have been traveling a road toward healing, believing that I am nearly "done" on several occasions, only to find out I am still near the beginning. Or perhaps it is a spiralling journey. I have falsely believed there is an ending, a time when I will no longer mourn or miss my mom. I am finding out that there is still pain too deep for words.

This past weekend, I told my story to a group of friends. It felt like I'd been tricked—I signed up for a workshop on relationships and was asked to talk about the year I was twelve. The leaders could have chosen any other year of our lives. But there it was: I was almost twelve when my mom died, so I had to tell that story.

My husband and I signed up for this workshop expecting a series of exercises that would enrich our connections with each other and with our children. I knew there were communication skills involved, but how that played out was shocking and upsetting...and revealing and healing.

We spend the first day of the workshop discussing the skills we will be practicing, and building trust within our small group of three couples and the leaders. To prepare for our "homework" on the first evening, the leader shows us how to draw our "genogram." This simple diagram uses symbols and lines to show how we perceive our family relationships at age twelve. The leader draws his own genogram, and I imagine mine. It dawns on me that I will have to draw my family relationships as they were in my "bad year"...the year my mom vanished from my life a few weeks before my birthday. On the genogram she will have a stroke through her symbol indicating her death—the thought of this unravels the reserves that normally hold me together.

I start to cry as the instructions for the genograms are given. I don't think I can do this; I can't talk about how bad that year was for me. I have a question, and as I look up to ask it, I notice another woman in meltdown. She too is about to face her most terrible year.

During the break she and I admit to each other that we both can say "that was the worst year of my life." For her, a sibling died. Her husband faces his own dark story; we all have different unbearable losses. What we share is the terrible knowledge that when a soul leaves this earth, a black hole is left behind, a hole in the soul of every family member. A black hole of pain cuts through you, with no answers for why half your heart disappeared. And no idea about how or if it will ever come back.

I prepare my genogram that evening. We've been warned that it might take an hour to draw it. I can draw my genogram in two minutes. I don't know any of my dad's family, his siblings or parents. I saw them four years before I turned twelve, and I don't know them well enough to draw a relationship line indicating a connection to them. I don't even draw a line to the uncle who came to stay with us for the weeks that coincided with that terrible loss. I feel no relationship with him in my year of being twelve. I don't know any of my mom's siblings or their children well either. I have only met them once, so I don't draw lines of connection to them.

I draw my nuclear family. I have a single line to my older sister Anna which means I consider our relationship superficial at this age. I draw a dotted line to my dad; the dotted line means I am distant from him. This is how I feel about them—barely connected.

I should have double lines to my mom, and she would have double lines to my dad and Anna as well, indicating strong, supportive relationships. But instead, she has a single stroke, a diagonal line, through her symbol. I have to put it there, and I draw her symbol with this line through it in the first thirty seconds. I know that marking her death with that single stroke could tear my heart apart. I draw quickly to avoid an eruption of emotions.

I go to bed. In the morning, I will tell my story and answer questions. I will have to describe the relationships that met important emotional needs—attention, affection, approval, and comfort—during that year. I'm afraid to prepare: afraid the pain will swallow me. If I plan my words ahead, it will be impossible to speak them.

I feel an ominous cloud of blackness descending, but I know the time has come to share my story, and these are people I can trust. An old friend of mine is leading the workshop, and when she checks in with me in the morning I feel the warmth of her support. I will be able to talk, and in the talking there will be tears. I know the sharing and tears will be one more step toward healing. I tell myself I am ready to share my bad year with trusted friends.

I start by explaining that at age twelve I lived in South America, and my parents' families lived in distant worlds, New Zealand and Canada. It is not hard to see why I had no relationships with any of them. My grandmother was just a name and the arrival of a monthly aerogram written in shaky handwriting that only my dad could decipher.

I explain how close my mom's death was to my twelfth birthday. I find I cannot speak the words, "She died." I wish I could wail, sob, and break apart, but that is far too unsafe. I warn the group that my presentation will be emotional. When the tears start running down my face, I reassure them that I am not going to come apart. I learned long ago that it is vitally important not to make people feel awkward and uncomfortable with my sorrow.

I finally say the words. "My mom died six weeks before my twelfth birthday." My voice catches, I sob, and I stop talking. I stab at my heart with logic, and I crumple the severe pain into its safe place. If I were to truly grieve, we would just stop here and cry for an hour or two.

My husband sits closer and holds my shoulder. He is strength to me, but I am still facing this alone. I know it is time. It is time to talk about this bad year in my life. I just need a moment to reorder my inner world.

To quell the rising tsunami of grief inside me, I choose another topic, a safer topic—my grade seven teacher. This part of the story defies rational explanation and ironically it lifts me out of the pain. Each Monday morning when our class arrived at school, we found our desks arranged into a new order, in a square. It took a few weeks for us to decipher the code, but we got the subtle message.

The best student of that week was seated at one end, descending down to the lowest student of the week at the other end. Unfortunately, I was in the top three every week, which made me a target for resentment. I had to do not-quite-my-best-work so I wouldn't be hated.

Despite my efforts to keep this fragile equilibrium with my peers, I was the brunt of an abrupt dismissal from a friendship I valued. I agonized over what I did to earn this rejection and begged her to tell me. When I talked to her, it was as if I were invisible. She wouldn't look at me or talk to me. Perhaps it was the desk rivalry, or maybe she couldn't stand the dark sorrow I carried around in silence. After she abandoned our friendship, I spent the year without any friends at school. The other girls, the pretty girls of the class, were in a clique that I tried to join, but they didn't want me either. I can tell this to the group without dissolving, and it helps pull my head and heart together.

I tell the group in our workshop that my parents were in Canada when my mom died, and I was at home with Anna and a visiting uncle and aunt. I tell them about the memorial service but not how I felt that day. Telling this story is a balancing act. I'm choosing what I can say without falling apart, calculating each admission for whether it will take me back to the choking silence of my first few minutes of sharing.

I tell them about the day Carol found me and I cried so hard I thought I was going to come apart, like a go-cart traveling too fast down a mountain and all the bolts come out and the wheels fly off and get lost. There was no chance of putting the go-cart back together, and the memory of this moment, the sobbing, is primal. I just say,

"I scared myself by crying too hard, so I buried the grief and never cried again."

I tell them about my mom's Australian friend, Milly. In a stroke of genius, God has made my best friend in this circle on this day also Australian. I feel comforted by her accent. I tell them that Milly's brother died on the same day as my mom. In our shared grief, Milly and I spent time together, but we didn't talk about our lost people. I tell them the story of visiting Milly after school each day, of avoiding my empty house, and of the things we did together, baking and sewing. We made a lavender skirt out of an old bridesmaid's dress my mom had made, but we didn't talk about that. We were companions, but we didn't travel a pathway built from words.

I tell them about losing Milly too, before the year was over. Not to death, but to jealousy when my dad got remarried. I was forbidden to talk to Milly. Not only was she gone from my life, but I felt terrible guilt at causing her more pain by abandoning her, too ashamed to tell her why.

Next I need to share about how my emotional needs for attention, affection, approval, and comfort were met during that year. I got some attention from Milly for the first part of the year, but the other needs were not met, not as they are defined within this seminar. After my father remarried, these needs continued to be unmet. My stepmother was focused on my deficiencies. Any expectation of approval or affection slowly died inside me. There was a tenuous relationship teetering between us, unable to flourish. She fed it with her need to control life and teach me things I should already know. I starved that relationship with an almost-polite silence.

I tell this group about my dad and the orange cassette player. I can say that, but I cannot tell them about the other gift. My dad also gave me a photo of my mom, a big 8" x 10" of her smiling face, beaming on the day she completed matching outfits for Anna and me to wear to the year-end assembly. It was the last time I remember her feeling well, and I had my own picture of it. But the photo disappeared from my room after my dad got married, and I was afraid to ask about it. I don't tell this story on this day to these friends because it will take me too close to the edge of the abyss. It makes one too many losses to talk about.

I also cannot tell this group about my dog. They might think it is trivial, but it isn't. When my dog died, I came out of a fog and into a sharp awareness that anyone around me could suddenly be gone—there was a chance I could be even more alone. This fear gnawed at the hole in my soul, making it bigger. Today as I tell my friends the story, I am too close to that familiar old feeling, the black hole of despair that threatened to swallow me when I was twelve. I cannot tell it all. Today, the hole has swallowed my energy, but it has not swallowed me.

The story has not been offered to these friends in an orderly fashion, but I think it is clear. I lost my mom, and my family disappeared into a fog, barely talking to each other, definitely not grieving together. I lost my best friend, and then my mom's best friend, and I lost my mom's other friends and community when my dad got remarried to someone who preferred a different social circle.

I had no idea how hard it would be to say this aloud. It was harder than I imagined, but better than I could have hoped. I feel drained, but it is good. The buried toxins have started to pour out from their hidden cave, and I know I've faced a barrier that needed to be broken.

The group asks some questions—they are careful with their words. We are practicing the skill of sharing emotions, and they comment on what they rejoice in, as well as on what they sorrow for, with me.

My Australian friend sits with her head down, tears running down her cheeks. No one has ever heard my story like this, with so many details. Not even I have looked at it in this light, adding up the layers and layers of loss, and observing that the basic relational needs of attention, affection, comfort, and approval were overlooked by the adults in my world.

It is a comfort, I find, to see that it breaks my friend's heart to listen to my story. After years of silence, and multiple conversations where I've been told to "get over it" and get on with life, her compassion is healing. Her tears are powerful, validating the times I have struggled to get beyond people's lack of understanding, lack of compassion, and sometimes heartless cruelty. She communicates that I was right in wanting to be understood. Today, for the first time, I am fully convinced that I am no longer alone. It is impossible to tell my story like this to a group of friends and still feel alone. I am convinced that my vulnerability has made a difference. If someone in the future tells me my story is not worth hearing, I will have this day as a plumb line to measure their words—not true. My story is significant.

As much as it hurts to tell the story, the pain is being released, and I feel that a burden I have carried has been distributed and carried by friends. It is shared by a community that has cried my tears with and for me, literally.

Their comfort is specific. I have shared that I cannot remember anyone hugging me during that year. One of the men says to me, "It breaks my heart that no one hugged you that year. I wish I could go there to your 12-year-old self. I would hug you." This is his comfort, rich in kindness, and like my friend's tears it helps my heart heal.

This is a hard day, going back and walking through all the loss. I am startled by how fresh the wounds feel, from what took place so long ago. When my mom died, a crater was blown through the centre of my life. It felt like a hole in my soul, the pain as black as ink. I thought it might consume me, devour my very existence. The emotion, the overwhelming nature of this loss, was so threatening that I buried it. But the black hole that consumed joy was still there. I knew every time I came near it that it was not gone, even after healing started.

Today I have stepped through that hole, as if I stepped from a cave into the passageway that leads toward the light. The combination of opportunity and compassion gave me the courage to make this step. I could choose to stop here and not continue toward the light—there is a certain risk to that journey. But intuitively I know this is the time in my life to journey: to write, to reflect, to talk. And to cry. I have done plenty of crying today and I will cry until I can talk again—I know that tears carry the gift of cleansing. They won't remove the pain, but they will remove the barriers to joy.

Going back to the memories that are crammed into this one year of my life has another side to it, which I had never stopped to ponder and consider. The losses in this year are much greater than I recognized when I looked at it alone, without friends asking questions and offering care. There are layers and layers of loss, additional pain buried in the same hole of silence. I am starting to see these as pieces of a puzzle; put together, they form a picture. That picture is of loss—but behind the loss there is what was lost. *It had to be there for me to lose it.* I had never stopped to think about that.

This group has held my rope, my safety net that allowed me to pass through the black hole. Now they have one more job to do. They are also "commissioned" to express their gladness at all the good things that my mom represents. There is joy in her loving gifts to me and celebration of her ability to embrace life and gift so many people with rich friendship. It is hard for me to hear them talk about this joy and celebrate her this way. But in this conversation, I begin to understand something I have never seen before. For everything good in my life before I was twelve, there is a loss, an absence of something that was good. *The sorrow is so great because there was so much to lose*. Their sadness for me is not lessened by their gladness—it is a genuine gift. But their gladness opens the door for me to recognize that grief is the expression of great love lost.

I have gained by telling them my story. I've taken a step toward being able to find joy in all the good that was in my life, and lost. A step toward living, more fully living, fulfilling my own life. Living in the light.

⁂ She Sings for Me ⁂

. . . . . .

February 1983 ~ Ellen

A decade has passed since my mom's death, but I am still young—just entering adulthood. I have buried the grief and not found healing, but I don't understand or fully realize how much of my reality includes this lurking darkness of buried pain and unexpressed grief. I am in college, and a classmate (not someone I know well) goes through an experience similar to mine, with younger sisters at home and a brother aged twelve. Their mom is sick for a few months, longer than my mom was ill. They know she has cancer, but the treatment is helping. We pray diligently as a school community for this mother to survive. It reminds me of my own story. Quite suddenly, outside of the doctor's expectations, she is gone.

We go to the mother's funeral. All of our class, the girl's classmates and I, are there.

I have never been to a funeral in Canada, and I can't remember being to one since my mom died. I have no idea what to expect, and I sit near the back knowing that I need the distance to protect me from disintegrating.

The funeral professionals wheel in the coffin, and the procession of family members follows. I am shocked. It is a parade, and the processional aspect reminds me of a wedding. It is foreign to me and seems bizarre and hideous, parading the coffin like this.

I start to cry, and I cannot stop—it is as if I am at my own mother's funeral, yet not.

There is no comfort for me in the grief I am experiencing. I know I am re-living my own grief, but the healing that tears should bring evades me. I know I have to offer comfort to my not-quite-a-friend. I know it is entirely possible that no one else in our class will know what to say, and she will feel alienated by awkwardness. This day is for her, not for me.

And so we become friends. Not good friends, but she knows I will listen and ask. I hear about her mom's fragile body, almost starved before she died. She tells me how this memory of her mother's gaunt body has come back again and again to taunt her. I don't mind the details, they don't raise my own grief—that moment has passed. I know this sharing is part of my friend's healing. I know other people are afraid of the horrors of this story, and I can give the gift of listening and being present in her sorrow.

My grandfather, my mom's dad, dies a few months later, and my sister and cousin and I are all wishing to go to his funeral. My cousin has a friend who will drive us, and we take the weekend and a day off school to get there and back, twenty hours each way. We have time in the car to prepare for the worst.

Will I survive? I don't know. Will I disintegrate? I am afraid I might experience the same overwhelming grief that flooded through me at the funeral a few months ago. But it is worse to be alone, to not go, and to not say good-bye. My grandfather has been a cherished link to memories of my mom.

The lesson from the last funeral is new and not yet fully clear, but I have understood that grieving for the "wrong thing" doesn't help. But I also know I cannot control the great darkness inside of me—sometimes it emerges when I don't want it to, and I'm afraid this will be one of those times. My grandfather's grave is beside my mom's. She was buried in her parents' town, now a long time ago in my mind.

Surprisingly, the funeral is bearable, and though I cry, it is for my grandfather and not for my unhealed wounds. When the relatives have dinner together, and we joke about his grouchy disposition and share our stories, it is normal and real, and I feel surprised by how natural this feels. We are grieving together, remembering the good with the bad. Sharing the pain of loss and the joy of remembering what we cherished about him.

After dinner we go to my grandfather's trailer home, and my aunt looks through his belongings. She finds a box of cassettes in the cupboard over the front window. She chooses one that is a recording of my mom singing —a cassette my dad sent her parents when we lived so far from them. There is an expectation that we will play it.

I assemble my inner barriers as my aunt fumbles with the cassette player. I cannot afford to let my pain come out, it may consume me as I feared it would at the funeral. If I prepare myself, I will be safe.

A voice I have not heard for nearly ten years sings a melody that is as familiar as my own heartbeat. I heard my mom sing these words many times throughout my childhood. I can see her standing near the piano, my dad playing the music to her lead —

Why should I feel discouraged?
Why should the shadows come?
Why should my heart be lonely,
and long for heav'n and home?
When Jesus is my portion?
My constant Friend is He:
His eye is on the sparrow,
and I know He watches me;
His eye is on the sparrow,
and I know He watches me.

Her voice lifts on the refrain to sustain a sweet, hopeful high note—"His eye is on the sparrow"—she holds the note in a pause. My heart fills at the sight of her—in my memory. Her voice drops back down and then rises again on the word "know"—"I know he watches me." Her certainty in this phrases holds me—grips me—with this question: Is God really watching me? She seems to have the answer.

Tears threaten to squeeze into this moment. I stifle the pain, my thoughts wrestling with emotions—a struggle to keep the lid on Pandora's Box. I will not let the flood open up this dam of pain. I cannot. My will holds tight and we move on to other conversation, but my thoughts turn over the choice of songs. The words echo and replay in my mind.

It feels arranged. God knows which song I needed to hear, and my mom's voice reaches into my soul with a promise. I am watched: the God who watches over sparrows is with me. I think of this often over the next few weeks, and I am grateful.

I still cannot open the box, but there is a ray of light that I can enjoy from this memory. Clearly this song is what I am meant to remember about my mom.

I return to my college with this cassette in my possession, but I cannot listen to my mom sing again. I keep the cassettes I have been given from my grandfather's collection in a box, unopened. More than twenty years pass before I listen to her voice for a second time.

⁜ July 2013 ~ Ellen ⁜

On this second occasion, I listen to the cassette of my mom's memorial service with my sister. The songs and prayers are not familiar to me. Most of them do not touch me in a deep place, but they raise the sorrow of a dark day closer to my emotional surface and leave me with a little bit less buried, hidden pain.

After we listen to the memorial tape, my sister and I play another cassette that I have found. There is a terribly muffled recording of my mom talking to her dad on the phone when my sister and I are infants; we figure out that her mom, our grandma, was ill, and she had called to check on her. I'm not sure why my dad would have taped this, but he did. He was probably playing with a new recording gadget, a novelty item in the 1960s.

We turn the cassette over, and my mom is singing another song. I have not heard this song for years. It is again like a messenger arranged for me to hear just the words I should be hearing to complement her memorial tape. I have an eerie feeling inside. A place that has rattled with an empty echo is being filled with her song.

She has a sweet voice, a clear pure sound: simple, not heavy with training. It is lovely to listen to, pure and tender. And so familiar, still after all these years of silence. And finally I realize why every time my mom sang, people commented on the quality of her voice, so often saying the same thing, which didn't make sense to me as a child. She sounded normal to me because I heard her singing nearly every day.

But today I understand their admiration. She had a uniquely sweet and pure voice, with a tenderness toward God that came through her songs. And my mom sings, as if it is just for me, on this cassette—

By and by, when I look on His face.
Beautiful face, thorn shadowed face.
By and by, when I look on His face,
I'll wish I had given him more.
(Grace Reese Adkins, 1948)

What more could my mother have given to God? How can she say this? *She gave it all.*

These words challenge me—I know I do not sing this song in my daily life. I am haunted by these words as I prepare to return to North Africa. Again, the song turns over and over in my mind as I pack up my house to leave.

I am giving up my proximity to my two grown children, ages 20 and 22. That is hard enough for me. My mom sings this song from the other side of eternity and tells me in this old, taped song, that whatever I give Him, it is for His glory, and it will all be safe. Juxtaposed against the songs and prayers and a sermon we cannot listen to in her memorial service, she sings, "I'll wish I had given Him more".

It is a message that I need to hear, and the song plays over in my mind for weeks and changes my inner world, for good. She is still my legacy, the one who influences me toward God in the most remarkable ways.

Long gone. Not forgotten.

⁂ The Singing Bird ⁂

. . . . . .

⁂ 1998 ~ Ellen ⁂

My husband and I have recently moved to North Africa. Living here for just under two years, we have found life challenging, but we are making our home here. For me, living as a foreigner has an ironically familiar sense of being "home." And having my own children has given me a new place to start building traditions and festivities that create the fabric of our family and home, the things that weave us together. I feel the empty spaces in my life being filled with the celebrations and milestones as our family grows.

Sometimes the buried grief of my past invades my life in unexpected and undeciphered ways. I am oblivious to how many tentacles it has attached to my everyday life.

We have three children, and the youngest is still tiny. I have to keep them all alive—I feel the weight of the responsibility to clothe and feed them and care for their health. I am also intensely aware that their lives should be rich in all the treasures of being loved. Treasures that I enjoyed as a child, then lost. My life is a litany of choices that I hope will create this cocoon of love around them.

Since my husband and I barely have enough money for groceries most months, there is no danger of spoiling the children with belongings. It is very much a case of wanting to give them the best of my attention and affirmation and tenderness.

The older two children want a pet. When they find a ladybug, they make a home for him in a jar, with no air. We sit on our back step and discuss at length what this is best for the bug, and whether he will manage to live at all in that jar, even if they bring him grass every day. Tearfully, they set the ladybug free. I realize how badly they want this pet, any pet.

I want them to have a pet, especially if it is important to them. I wouldn't mind a dog, but it seems out of reach in a country where dogs are not considered pets. The children decide they would like a bird. A bird feels like extra work to me, and I'm concerned I won't have the capacity to give it daily attention. So I have a discussion with my husband.

My husband and I talk about whether it might be good for the children to have a pet. The reasons we list include teaching them to give consistent care to something. And we feel, yes, it would be good—besides, they keep on begging. Persistence should sometimes be rewarded.

I have one big fear: that this bird will die under my care. I tell my husband about my fear, and I tell him that I don't have the inner reserves to take care of one more thing. I take care of the household—him and my children—I cannot carry responsibility for one more living being.

He agrees to supervise. He will make sure the kids watch that the bird gets food and water. So long as we have this agreement in place, I am delighted to get a bird for the kids. In my mind, my husband will now be responsible if the bird dies, and that is enough.

The children choose a delicate little yellow canary. My husband comes through the front door carrying her cage. The kids dance around him, admiring her beauty. When she sings, I feel like a ray of sunlight is flooding our house. If sunlight could be a song, she sings its melody. Her music is magical, a blessing. The kids are happy; each morning her song fills the house with an invitation to joy. I fall in love with their canary.

But they are too little to take note of her water levels and her food without prompting. My husband is, predictably, a little absentminded. Sometimes I have to remind him of our agreement. When I do, he keeps his side of the bargain. This is just one step away from me being responsible, which is barely okay. I am managing, but the slope is steep, and the sand is sliding beneath my feet.

We go away for the weekend and are worried that the bird will run out of food and water in her containers while we are gone. We fill them up and give her to a friend to watch over her while we are away for two days. We give him instructions to keep the water tube filled.

When we come home, the water tube is completely empty, but no one notices—it looks the same when it is full: no water line. Our family arrives home in the evening; a late supper and bedtime routines consume our energy. We are busy with our three little ones, and my mind is not clear enough for this detail about the water. My husband has probably forgotten the bargain we made, and the bird is just a bird—to him.

I feel unsettled in the evening, and something is wrong. The bird is trying hard to get out of her cage, frantic for freedom. I fail—again—to take in that the water tube is empty. I reassure myself that she must be unsettled from moving back and forth, from house to house.

In the morning she is dead, and, of course, the kids and I see the empty water tube.

My husband has left for work before we notice her —he leaves the house at 7:00 a.m. on Mondays.

The kids are upset. This is their pet. Their grief is real, if temporary. I have a hard time biting my tongue, refraining from speaking my thoughts. I want to shout at them for not being more responsible and doing their part. I stifle bitter words of blame, but the anger burns inside of me.

The terrible part is that I am far more upset than they are. Yes, they are sad. But I am devastated.

I step outside, where they can't see me, and my tears flood out in sobs. I weep for this little bird who needed water so badly she nearly crushed herself to get out of her cage. My grief is a storm of emotions.

I don't understand this. She was a beautiful little bird, and I loved to hear her sing, but this overwhelming sadness, this flood of tears, is disproportionate to everything and anything that makes sense to me.

I thought it would be my husband's fault if she died, and I would be safe from this horrible grief and the guilt.

Nothing about this day makes sense to me. Not yet.

⁂ A Boatload of Barnacles ⁂

. . . . .

The thing that continues to intrigue me about healing is how it reveals secrets after the fact. Many, but not all, of the things that have changed as I have travelled into the mystery of healing have been surprises. Often I have dealt with emotional pain and found that something I thought was "normal" or part of my personality became clearer, or free-er, in the healing process.

For many years I avoided sitting beside the window on airplanes. I didn't avoid getting on airplanes, so I would have denied that this was a problem. I only felt panic for the first two minutes of takeoff and flight, then the fear subsided. So I would not have called this a phobia or panic disorder. But when the fear stopped, suddenly and without any obvious connection to having talked about it, or prayed about it, I realized that it had been hanging on to me like a barnacle on a boat. One or two barnacles don't sink a boat, but a boatload of them will.

Healing, for me, has been a slippery and elusive pursuit. I had to reach desperation before I was ready for the risk it would take to open the Box, Pandora's Box of terrific pain. Keeping that box lid on tight had kept me safe for so many years, I believed it was the best way forward without knowing that was even a belief. Finally there was a tipping of the scales, and the well-secured box began to destroy me, or more specifically, it began to destroy my family. The desperation that rose up with that realization pushed me toward healing.

I tried, at first, to get help that was safe, anonymous. Prayer for vaguely-worded needs, with a wide possibility of interpretations was my first chosen cry. It may be that these prayers helped more than I thought, but this didn't seem to create a measurable change. However, when I reached the point of being willing to do anything, reveal anything, in order to be free of my destructive patterns, then I began to find healing in a measure that changed my inner world.

I can tell you exactly where I was when the healing process became real and active for me—that day when the choice to risk anything trumped the prior decisions that had kept me safe.

I was in a hotel in Turkey, a short flight from my North African home.

⁜ November 2000 ~ Ellen ⁜

We are attending a conference with the church that sends and supports us in our work. Our leaders are here, but the real support comes from our community of friends in the church. The closest of these friends have a daughter we've grown to love. She has suffered immeasurable grief, although she is only in her early twenties. Engaged to be married, she finds out her fiance has cancer. With their infant son in her arms, she buries her husband less than two years later. She tells me about her effort to write poetry as a means of expressing her grief—she hopes her book of poems will help other young widows. We share a common understanding of loss, and she shows me the poetry.

I am not an accomplished poet, but she has never heard of personification in poetry, so I try to explain it. She still doesn't understand, so I decide to write something as an example of this. I write about the moment my uncle gives me the news of my mom's death, with the wind dancing through my curtains. I have no idea writing this will unravel my inner world as rapidly and completely as it does. I am suddenly bathed in the primal emotions of loss, awash with grief that has aged and intensified in its silent casks beneath the surface of my busy life.

I find myself sobbing—sobbing in a swirl of grief that embarrasses and shames me. Although I am alone in my hotel room with my sleeping children, I am here in Turkey, among the very people who have told me to "get over it." These leaders have pushed me to be a "better" Christian, a stronger witness, a more emotionally efficient minister of the gospel—to give a stronger performance on the stage of life.

I have come apart, and in my own eyes, through this imposing lens, I am a failure.

Simultaneously I am in a season where I am acutely aware of my secret defeat in the area of anger. I have a pattern of yelling at my children when they fail to listen to me. Their childish behaviour seems outrageously wrong. Looking back, their behaviour is normal, but in my chaos, I think I need to get them to behave more appropriately. I am easily angered when I don't establish the "right" level of obedience in our home.

It doesn't occur to me on this warm evening in a Turkish hotel room, with the children soundly sleeping while I write my memories and sob in pain, that the anger

I fear in myself and my hidden grief share a common root. That revelation will come within a few months.

Although I am ashamed and frustrated by this episode of grieving, I am able to cry. It has been years and years since I have cried with sorrow for my mom's death. It feels like I am spending every emotional penny I have on tears. When I am spent, I wash my face, get into bed, and sob quietly a few more times before falling asleep.

In the morning, cold water splashed on my face and determined effort get me to the breakfast table without the telltale signs of this gripping episode of grief. I am aware that a storm is brewing inside, but I am maintaining control of the flimsy sailboat in this building squall.

As I step into the elevator alone, having left my children with their caregivers, I hear a voice in my head. Startled, I stop and listen again. It is not an audible voice, I don't turn to see if I am really alone. But it is a voice that is clear and distinct from my own thoughts, and it cannot be ignored. It sounds like a voice in my memory, repeating verbatim a phrase that was spoken to me, literally, physically, the previous day. It has that kind of clarity. It is either God speaking to me, or Satan tempting me to believe a lie, but the latter is usually much more subtle than this.

As I ride up to the top floor, alone in the elevator, I am increasingly aware that I am not alone. Crisply, one simple thought turns and repeats inside my head. It is a phrase that I will ponder and compare to my understanding of Truth for several weeks to come. *"It is not the events of our lives that wound us. It is the broken relationships that cripple us and break our hearts."*

I think that this statement refers to the breaking of the relationship with my mom, through her sudden death.

This loss is the epicentre of my pain. But years later I can see that it is referring to a much bigger circle of relationships impacted by her death and the subsequent reinventing our family on broken foundations.

When the elevator reaches the top floor, I enter into the conference room where a gentle time of worship and closeness to the Father is underway. I feel invited into a renewed, deeper beauty in being vulnerable with God. It is cleansing. I am fully honest with Him about how broken I am and about how the broken relationships in my family have crippled my heart. I find a way to give this to Him, surrendered in an offering of both mourning and praise, allowing God to be inside my secrets of anger and pain.

I feel new hope in the presence of the God who longs to be my companion—a Father who longs to comfort me. And I am moved toward healing. I think I am the one who is moving—toward God, toward healing, toward hope. But it is the other way around. God has pursued me, through all my troubled years. He has been present and, like a shepherd behind me, has been herding me toward a relationship that will allow me to heal in His love. I just have to say "yes" in complete honesty. And surrender.

This has been a step toward that place of sharing my dark sorrow with Him and it was made possible by the essential discovery of the true nature of Pandora's Box. When I was a child, it felt as if the contents I buried there were dangerous and uncontrollable, and *maybe that was true because I was still a child.*

As an adult I am able to deal with the darkness I've hidden, and there are two things I have learned about my own personal Pandora's Box. First of all, the contents of that box will not destroy everything in my world if I take the lid off and let the darkness out. I will survive this rupturing of my protective lid. And secondly, it is not true that you cannot put things back inside the box. I can and will let out the pain a bit at a time, but I can also go back to covering it up when I need to. There is no conscious awareness of this, but the experience of it has begun.

Though I don't know it yet, my Father has begun to prepare a table for me, in the presence of this dark pain in my soul.

⁂ Humpty Meets The King ⁂

. . . . .

⁂ 1993-2000 ⁂

My children are my greatest joy in life. They are also my greatest source of frustration, annoyance, and distress. I enjoy their never ending energy, and usually their antics. But they don't listen carefully to what I tell them, and they don't usually follow my directions the first time, and this, quite often, is too much for me to accept. I am in my first years of parenting, and I am discovering that I am not as adequate as a mom as I thought I would be. It's not a simple matter of teaching obedience with patience. Parenting is not nearly simple enough.

Admittedly, there are great moments of tenderness and love and closeness and laughter. These are a treasure to my heart. I want every day to be like this—all day. But I am a disappointment to myself.

There are too many terrible moments—moments when a flood of emotion blows through my gates of reserve, and I blast the not-listening child with a fiery hell of anger that they certainly don't deserve.

I hate myself for these moments, even though there are more good days than there are bad ones. This sad calculation of weight on each side does nothing to console or acquit me. I've been hiding this terrible secret about myself because I am worried that someone will tell me I am not worthy of these amazing children.

After five or six years of determined effort, it has become obvious that private prayer, self-help books, and vows of self-control are not going to fix this problem. I am starting to get desperate, which feels a lot like despair—but is not.

In despair, I've struggled to not give up. In desperation I've become more thirsty for the answer to my prayers, but also more prepared for whatever form the answer takes. God knows I have asked Him for help many times, and help is on the way, just not in the silent miracle that I hoped for.

I have been brought up to believe that Jesus is the Saviour of the world. The crux of this teaching is that if I believe and surrender to Christ, He will forgive my sin, and I will not spend eternity in hell. My daily pursuit of this truth is to find what is wrong with myself and ask for forgiveness so I can be better, do better. The focus in my walk of faith is on me. I need to improve at living with perfect patience, kindness, gentleness, and self-control. But that is not my reality. If this is a race, I am not winning any prizes.

In my head, I also know that this is not the whole truth about Jesus, with nothing left out. I know I am supposed to be living the abundant life of God's promises in this world of here and now. Unfortunately, I have no idea how to access that, beyond finding what is wrong with me, which most often isn't too hard.

Here's what is missing: although I have gone to a Christian college where they recite the words "Jesus is our Healer," I have not experienced that for myself. I believe this promise might work for the healing of my body, if I am ill. That Christ's presence might heal my soul—heal my inner darkness that I've hidden in lock-down—is a foreign thought.

⁜ January 2001 ⁜

I am at a winter conference: this one is held in a monastery in the mountains. I am cold all day and all night, which distracts from just about everything—except the speakers. Their message engages my whole being, and I forget how cold it is as I sit and listen. They share their own stories of healing for emotions, describing the way hidden wounds and suppressed pain get the better of us. For the first time I understand that beyond my sin, my buried pain has put barriers between my inner self and God. I immediately see the connection between my outbursts of anger and deep roots of buried grief for my mom, which I have accessed at the conference before this one.

The couple teaching are giving four seminar lectures, but they offer to do a session demonstrating how to pray this way for healing. They will only do this if there is someone willing to take the risk and be their "guinea pig." The other participants will watch. I have no idea that between all the sessions they are also doing private prayer for people who ask and for those who find this request too public.

In the past few months, I have grown desperate. I know the anger issues need to be resolved. I know the pain over my mom's death is still deep inside, and I know my prayers for magical changes in my explosive world have not helped. I don't care if the whole conference watches, I just want to be set free of destructive outbursts that have been shadowing my family life.

On the break, before anyone is out the door, I am at the front, volunteering to receive prayer. I erroneously believe it is my only chance to get their personal help at the conference.

The afternoon session is a two-hour slot, and I am asked to sit in the central chair, while they "do" my prayer as a demonstration. I know from the morning's lecture that we will ask Jesus to bring back a memory and meet me there, in that memory. The leaders expect Jesus to show Himself present and to have a conversation with me. This part of the prayer is easy for me. I have a great imagination, and I have cultivated a daily conversation with Jesus. Even though I have plenty of issues I am ashamed of, I've never shied away from talking with Him about other ordinary requests. My conversations have been shaped by a book called *Practicing the Presence of God*, by Brother Lawrence.

As we begin the prayer session, I recall a situation with my mom when I was ten years old, and then a split second later another situation with my stepmother. I know these two memories are what Jesus is bringing to the surface for healing. The main person leading this prayer session, Jane, finishes her opening prayer and asks Jesus to bring back a memory, but I know He has already started that process. I tell her about the two memories I've just seen.

We easily fall into a rhythm. I tell Jane where I am in a memory, not leaving my place in the picture I have of that event in my imagination. As I describe it to her, I imagine myself, at that age, in the memory. She asks good questions to clarify when and where the memory comes from. Then she asks Jesus to show up. I look around, sometimes turning to see the whole room, and yes, I find He is there, usually standing not too far from me.

By keeping my eyes closed, I feel like I am inside a soap bubble—very light, weightless, and moveable, but prone to popping. I feel more anxious about the bubble popping than I do about the circle of people watching this session unfold. Jane then asks Jesus to converse with me. I can ask Him whatever I want to know, and He answers sometimes with words, but sometimes by changing how I feel about the situation.

These first memories, with my mom and stepmother, give Jane the historical context of my mom's death and my dad's remarriage. In the first memory, the conflict I feel is easily resolved, and I am reassured that Jesus is there to heal the disappointment I experienced. In the second memory, with my stepmother, I feel a great weight of shame. It is hard to admit to Jane the events that cause this, and it is hard to let go of the shame and the hurt. But I feel these emotions lifting when Jane prays for Jesus to touch my heart with healing. I am able to agree with Jane that I need to forgive my stepmother, and it is much easier to do that after Jesus has healed the pain.

We also go to some deeper hurts, places where the weight of the pain of death comes back to me like a boulder sitting between my shoulder blades, crushing my insides. I cannot speak audibly because the pain that I am feeling has taken my voice away. I am back in my childhood, back to the days before I learned to fold it all down into a box inside.

Jane has the good sense, or wisdom and guidance from the Holy Spirit, to pray a simple prayer for me each time this happens. Through four or five memories, I feel the boulder descend. I am speechless. She prays, "Jesus, come and heal this pain." As she prays this, the boulder lifts, and I can speak again.

The prayer time stretches past two hours in length. I am still in my bubble, afraid that if I open my eyes, all the mystery of this healing power will be gone. I have reentered my past, and Jesus is there, lifting off the terrifying, silencing pain. In case the opportunity never comes again, I want to take care of everything I can remember. We pray for two and a half hours. The final memory brings me healing in the least predictable way.

I recall a scene that is not real, or at least has never really happened. It has happened once before in my mind, at another time of prayer when someone tried a guided imaginary journey with me. I don't know if that journey had good results or not, it might have been the very first layer of healing. I don't want to discount it. In that journey, the man praying told me to visualize a cemetery, and my mom in it, with Jesus. In my imagination, she was a girl about twelve years old, with long white-blonde hair. She was lying limp in his arms. The person in charge told me to imagine Jesus taking her away with Him, so I did as I was instructed. But inside I was screaming "***NO. Don't go***!" I imagined the scene, but I didn't relinquish her. It tore my heart into pieces to see her go.

As this scene comes to mind on this occasion, I am wary that there is any healing to be had in this kind of imaginary picture. Although I can't discount it, I also know it didn't feel helpful the last time.

Throughout this prayer session, Jane has asked Jesus to be the guide for what I think, remember, and imagine. I see this same scene: Jesus holding my mom as a young girl. It has come back to me because Jane asked Jesus to show me what He wants me to see.

Again my mom is limp in the arms of Jesus, probably sleeping since she is not a dead, stiff body.

Jesus is seated on my mom's gravestone. I can see them, but I am not near them. Jane asks the same question, only it is a question, not a directive. Can I let Jesus have her, take her to heaven?

I have gained some confidence through these two hours of healing. My honesty about the memories and how I feel in them has been crucial to this process. I have gained confidence that I am allowed to speak what is truly in my heart. When Jane asks this as a question, I answer truthfully.

"No, I can't do that." I am being honest with myself, as much as I am being honest with Jane. I have learned in the past to give the "right" answers. This strategy has often shielded me from someone's scorn, or misunderstanding or correction. Today I am bold—I tell the truth.

"Okay," says Jane. To my surprise, she has no argument or advice. She says in her gentle voice, "We will leave her here with Jesus. That is fine." And this is how the prayer time ends, with a completely unresolved issue. Yet Jane is quite calm, undisturbed. And I feel relief: I am allowed to be "unfinished."

When I reflect on the healing prayer session, I write about it for a friend, and I say—

"This moment when she lets me choose and say, "No, I'm not ready," this is the most healing thing that happened that day."

I'm not sure it is. The moments when the boulders lift off my shoulders are powerfully healing. That is the raw power of God changing my life. It isn't that the pain has magically disappeared. It is that the volcanic nature, the compression of darkness, has begun a process of disintegration.

And that is not the only powerful truth of this day. The discovery that Jesus was present throughout my life, spiritually in the room with me, during my lowest moments, caring for me—that is a whole new level of understanding in my faith. The capacity that God has to impact my emotional life and not just my ideas about who He is —this is new and life-giving to me.

It is perhaps the personal nature of this, the option to have an honest conversation about who I am and what I can and cannot do with my emotional landscape, that astounds me. I'm accepted with all my ugly baggage. And I feel loved despite my darkness.

Talking with Jane in this moment of freedom, the choice I have to be honest, or not, and the reaction of being accepted for my own weakness: this is the first time I have truly felt someone share my pain and accept that it is my reality. Jane has not put shame on me for failing to get over "it."

There will be more healing prayer times in the years ahead, but this prayer session changes the course of my life. It has a profound effect on my anger issues. I come to realize that my anger is not a reaction to injustice or a statement of right and wrong.

Anger is a valve for the stream of emotion that is buried deep inside me. I have channeled too much into my Pandora's Box, where I have to keep the lid from blowing off and the intense pain from shredding my heart. The anger is rooted in pain, and the pain is rooted in loss, and the loss is my broken world. I have felt helpless in this trap I made for myself as a child. That helplessness is gone, and with it the lie that none of this can change.

I am exactly what I was so afraid of becoming as a child. As I suspected, I am Humpty Dumpty. I fell off a wall, and the millions of pieces have not been put together again.

Today the process of rehabilitating my soul begins. Not because of my hard work and effort, and not because Jane is a magician. It isn't all the king's horses, or all his men that put me back together. That part is true—they cannot put me back together.

But the King can. This is only the beginning, but sometimes all you need to keep going is hope. And I have that now. From this day onward, I believe He will continue to heal me. There will be many more ups and downs, and the road will be longer than I could possibly imagine with speed bumps and potholes and hairpin turns. But through them all, I will have hope. Hope for healing.

When I get on an airplane to fly home three days later, I surprise myself by telling my children I would like to sit by the window. As we take off into a clear night sky punctuated with stars, I am thrilled by the view of city lights, rather than terrorized by the fear of death. My panic button has been demolished. I have this moment, this good memory cementing the knowledge: healing has begun.

⁂ Another Child, Another Mother ⁂

. . . . . .

⁎ February 2009 ⁎

It is 2:00 a.m. in winter; the ringing of our phone wakes my husband and me from deep sleep. My husband is pulling on his clothing before he is even off the phone. It is a good friend, Hamed, who has called. Hamed's brother, Samir, has been killed in a car accident. Their family lives two hours away, but my husband will go; he is out of our driveway in minutes.

My husband is gone for two days, helping the family bury their youngest son, the one that makes them all laugh, the life of the party. The party that is now over. The grief is crippling.

Hamed's wedding is supposed to be in three months, but the culture dictates it will be postponed for a year. Or perhaps not, the family is in chaos, the death adding to their confusion and needs.

⁜ July 2009 ⁜

It is 2:00 a.m. again, five months have passed. I am at the wedding with our four children. Hamed has married, in a celebration that more closely resembled a wake than a wedding. The evening was marked with chanting instead of music, no dancing, and no highlights of joy or laughter. Hamed's mother asked that he not postpone his marriage because her arthritis is worse, and she can no longer cook. She needs a daughter-in-law to take over.

But Hamed's mom does not wear festive clothing for the evening, and neither do many of the guests. Photos are taken in private, without any of the usual jovial banter. Guests are somber, mostly silent, matching the morose strains in the music. It is a relief when the guests start to go home and the evening is finally done.

Now, into the night hours, my husband is chauffeur for the chanting band, normally hired for funerals and wakes. He is taking them home. They left before midnight, and he will soon be back; their village is just over an hour away. This is the first wedding we've attended that ended before midnight.

My younger daughter is falling asleep and asking if she can lie down. I take her to a room with mattresses on the floor. While she is settling, I hear the sound of a human voice, raised in a song of lament. I am startled and transfixed. I have heard such a voice in an opera performance, the sound of profound sadness, expressing deepest regret, deepest longing.

But this is different—the emotional overtones and undertones are all genuine, not a dramatic performance mimicking life. I recognize the song, even though I have never heard it before. If I had sung a lament for my mom when she died, it would have sounded like this.

It is sung in a language that I am familiar with, but the words are not clear. Only one phrase is perfectly clear to me, "Oh God, why have you taken my son from me?"

When I look down again, my daughter is sleeping soundly. I move quickly from this room toward the sound of the voice. My feet take me faster than my mind can think. My instincts have broken through any barriers of protocol, and I act without thought for whether I am being culturally appropriate. I've skipped the usual question: what should I do?

I see Hamed's mother sitting at the side of their large, bare courtyard where the wedding guests sat. It is summer, and the night air is pleasant after a scorching day and sweltering evening. Family members are sitting nearby enjoying the cooling air. Tears are still flowing down the bereaved mother's face, though the song has stopped before I get to her. No one moves to acknowledge or comfort her.

She needs a mother's embrace, a mother's comfort—my instincts tell me this. I gather her as if she is the size and shape of my sleeping child, and fold her into my arms with her head resting on my chest. I brush her hair gently and murmur the only words I trust in this moment, words that have brought me healing with consistency. "Jesus, come. Jesus, come. Jesus, heal her pain." She rests there, as if she knows I am offering her the safe place of her mother's arms, and though she doesn't hear or understand my prayer, I feel there is comfort flowing to her heart.

Moments pass, she gains her composure, we move on—naturally. There is no awkwardness between us. We understand the need for a broken heart to be held with tender care; this is a universal understanding between those who share such a grief as this.

Time passes, and my husband will be here momentarily. I go down to check on my daughter, passing the kitchen where Hamed's mother and some relatives are finishing putting things to rest for the night. An auntie speaks to me in a reprimand, telling me that I had no business comforting Hamed's mother the way I did. The time for mourning is over, the time for living is here. In this culture you don't offer comfort when the 40 days are over, it is weakness to do this.

I say nothing; I don't feel any need to defend myself. Hamed's mother speaks out firmly. "Don't say that to her. She did what was right. She held me, she cared for me. *I felt her tears on my cheek.* **She loves me.**"

I tell no one about this night, beyond a few words to my husband. For the next six months, this moment is too deep inside of me for sharing. Her pain has matched my own, and I realize I am still deeply in need of healing; time will allow for that. But for now, I need the silence, again, to protect me.

I experience on this night a profound emotion that I have never felt before. It is not that I feel this has equalized my loss, it is not that much. But I feel a new understanding of the verse that the Bible gives for the wounded—"we comfort with the comfort we have been given."

For five minutes, I have a slim satisfaction that the grief I have lived, the mourning I have been blessed with, and the healing I have experienced have given me—what? The skills? No, this is not a skill. The right? No, there is no "right" in this passage. The privilege? Yes, perhaps it is that. This dark moment of sharing the pain, and the ensuing brief gift of hope that I pass along to this woman in the comfort she feels of my tears on her face—this is a privilege. I bring her the hope of healing, and it is a privilege to be here to do this.

Nothing will ever make the loss I experienced worthwhile. But now I know there can be moments when I feel the mystery of redemption in it.

When my husband arrives we are quick to load into the van; we need to get home to bed ourselves. As he starts the engine, two nephews on the edge of the courtyard begin to cry, weeping aloud. They are now experiencing Hamed's mom's lament, in their own way—grieving their own loss of the young, laughing uncle who was the life of every party, save this one.

Their mother speaks sternly, admonishing them that this is not a time to cry. Hamed's mother, their grandma, steps up and stops her. "No," she says. "Their tears are right, let them cry." She comforts them, holds them. As a mother should.

I leave with that small token of satisfaction in my silent space. I will not be able to talk about this for weeks and months. But I know they will mourn and be healed, and I am glad I was there.

⁜ The Ball of Wax ⁜

. . . . . .

I have never gone back to visit the city that was "home" for fourteen years of my childhood. If I did go back now, Cochabamba would be a strange city, not the one I remember. But it was not the city that left a hole in my soul. It was the loss of my feeling of home. "Home" was the mountain that disappeared into the sea when my world was shaken with death. Then my stepmother came along with her own ideas of family and home, and she set out to reform our family, building on the watery ruins of our unshed tears.

When my mom died, we lived in silence for the next nine months, in a house that daily echoed our loss. When my dad remarried, my sense of being "at home" slipped between the many rules I could not keep and the hard words that expressed my stepmother's frustration with me. The words punished me more efficiently than the "fines" that were levied against my monthly allowance.

These pronouncements of my failings convinced me that I did not belong in my own family—I did not live up to these new expectations. The silent walls that had preserved a fragile economy of acceptance between my dad and sister and me were blown down by the verbalization of my stepmother's disappointments. This lack of personal success was a terrible secret I kept disguised behind a forced smile. My shame was a private curse, dictating a commitment to keep everyone out of my hidden place of failure.

I am sure if my stepmother were telling this story, her perspective would justify her disappointment, at least to some degree. But the brokenness of my heart proved to be a fertile place for anger to grow within me—toward her. Instead of arguing with her, or rebelling against her rules, I grew more silent. I managed to keep my anger within me, except for a few moments in the mornings, when I walked out onto the street, turned the corner and trudged toward the school bus stop. For the next few minutes, maybe two or three, I would scream insults, directed toward her. I didn't care what the neighbours might think. But I waited until I was no longer on our block because I cared enough for this not to be known in my own home.

⁜ July 2010 ⁜

There is a week in my life, in 2010, when God addresses my need for freedom from the terrible bitterness of losing my home and my father to the woman who is his wife. It is, ironically, a week of silence.

I am invited on a silent retreat by a friend who offers to pay the bill. I have never been on a silent retreat, so when I speak to the retreat director, she is worried. Most people cannot adjust to seven days of silence if they have never done a day and then a weekend first. This is how they prepare for the "shock" of a week of silence. She tells me she would normally just say no, but she will pray and ask God to give her the answer, and we hang up the phone. I expect she will say I can come, and I am right.

I have no idea what is considered normal to other people. I have nothing to tell me that my years of silence are far from most humans' experience. I arrive at the retreat and meet nine women. After supper we enter into silence. I've been warned that I will find myself restless, yearning for words and conversation. Since I am mostly an extravert, this is even more the expectation.

But it is not hard at all. I lie on my bed the first morning, listening to the birdsong outside and feeling the breeze of the fan in my room. It feels like the breeze is blowing through me, like I have no skin, no body. I am nothing but a soul. I am familiar with the silence, but not with this skinless sensation that I am invisible. Oddly, the invisible part is emotionally familiar. The silence isn't scary or upsetting, nor do I wish I could talk to someone. I feel at home.

Each morning I have a 30-minute talk with the director, who gives me ideas of what to read and pray about. I walk around a small lake each day; this walk takes 90 minutes. Others walking on the path are chatting loudly and incessantly with words that are obviously superfluous to their needs, filling up spaces where silence would serve them better. I am happy here in my silent cocoon.

I find a small, windowless chapel in the basement of the retreat centre, and I enter. With the door shut and the lights off, it is a place of blackness, and I feel enclosed and even safer as I spend a few hours here each day. I don't think anyone else is using this little chapel—whenever I pass by, it is empty. I spend more and more time here as the week goes on.

Over several days I experience a mental picture in this little chapel. As the images come back through my imagination, it is like remembering a scene from a movie I once watched and found quite engaging. In this image there is a large ball of wax, which is slowly melting, dripping slowly to diminish its size. The next day, when it is still smaller, I see a black thorn lodged inside of it. I know this ball is my heart.

My heart has begun the melting process in the moments that I have relaxed in the silent sanctuary of the dark little chapel. Suddenly I see that the ball is no longer wax but a type of special gem, not a crystal and not a diamond, but a gemstone. And the black thorn is gone; there is, in fact, no flaw in it. I look carefully for a flaw, and I cannot find one.

The next day as I watch, the gemstone is no longer clear and crystal-like. It is a ruby, a large, beautifully rich-red ruby. When I come back and look closely on the following day, I see my beautiful ruby set into a piece of jewelry—a ring.

Until now, this has been a reassuring picture, good things are happening, and I feel emotionally revived by this process. When I tell my director about this, and she asks about the black thorn that was lodged inside, we reach a moment of discomfort. She has given me a passage to pray about God's presence with me and His blessing on me. She has asked me to pray this passage with my name inserted into it, and to receive all the blessings of these promises for myself, personally. The passage is from Isaiah 43.

But now the Lord who created you, O Israel, says: Don't be afraid, for I have ransomed you; I have called you by name; you are mine.

When you go through deep waters and great trouble, I will be with you. When you go through rivers of difficulty, you will not drown! When you walk through the fire of oppression, you will not be burned up—the flames will not consume you.
For I am the Lord your God, your Saviour, the Holy One of Israel. I gave Egypt and Ethiopia and Seba to Cyrus in exchange for your freedom, as your ransom.
Others died that you might live; I traded their lives for yours because you are precious to me and honoured, and I love you. CSB

I feel the blessing and closeness of God as I go through this Scripture and prayer exercise. My heart finds rest in the stillness of being alone with these words. I tell my director that it has been a wonderful experience. But now, as she asks me about the thorn inside my ball of wax, that blessing is at risk. I tell her that the black thorn is the bitterness I still feel toward my dad's wife for her part in my life.

The director asks me if I can pray the Isaiah 43 passage over my stepmother as part of my prayers in the next twenty-four hours. Can I put my stepmother's name into it and bless her, the way I have been blessed?

I have a simple, honest answer for her: "No."

She asked if I could. And I can't.

The director realizes her mistake and apologizes. "I should not even have asked that of you," she admits. Then she asks me what it will take for my heart to heal from the pain that is under the bitterness. I tell her that I have no idea. I have spoken words of forgiveness through the grit of determined obedience. I have tried to find healing in many ways. And I am still here at this retreat working through bitterness. We decide to leave this discussion for tomorrow, and since our 30 minutes is over, that is the obvious decision. Perhaps after 24 more hours in my safe, silent cocoon I will be ready to talk about this.

I walk out the door and down a path for about fifty paces, aimlessly and with no plan to even make a plan. I have suspended the anticipation of outcomes for this one week, somehow. The silence and stillness have been my rescue from setting goals and measuring progress.

I enter a room and spy a stack of CDs. I look through them hoping to find something inviting. The other participants have brought music to create this CD library for our week together. Two people have brought the same CD with a title that engages me. I decide their double vote is enough: I will listen to this one.

I lie down on the floor and start the music, which is beautiful and soft and comforting. As I listen, I feel a strong sensation, like I did the first day when the breeze from the fan left me skinless. This time, the sensation is that the pain as well as the bitterness in my heart is melting into the floor around me, like the ball of wax I saw when I started this mental movie. It feels like a relief to let it melt, so I surrender to the music and the sensation. This feels so real, so physical, that I think about how the carpet around me should be encased in wax and ruined. I think it would be a large puddle of wax.

The mystery of God's presence and timing is the miracle of healing. He does what I cannot do and removes what is entrenched in my darkness. I cannot say why it happens this way on this day, but it does.

When the CD ends, I get up to go to lunch. The bitterness is gone.

It is a silent retreat, so I tell no one. This also seems right. I cannot say why.

During the last day of the retreat, I see the ruby ring again, for the first time in a negative scenario. The ring is now set into a circle of filthy rotten leaves, like cabbage leaves that are stinking and dripping with a revolting slime. I know this is the bitterness I have carried and the unforgiveness that has haunted me over these years. And now, free of the pain and bitterness, I am ready to forgive my stepmother.

I go through every offence I can think of, name it out loud, and say my stepmother's name, with the sentence "I forgive you for...."

As I speak each utterance of forgiveness, I can see a revolting cabbage leaf turning into a gold or silver leafy shape. The setting for the ruby ring is now crafted with exquisite beauty.

When I leave the week of silence, I walk away from an enormous burden of pain that is tied not to my mom's death but to her "replacement." I am free. Or free-er.

I have made more space for healing.

⁂ 39 Days from 12 ⁂

. . . . . .

⁂ June 2011 ⁂

Today was Sunday—Father's Day Sunday. We tried to have a barbecue and a walk, but the rain interfered, and now the throbbing of heavy drops on the roof and drainpipe are keeping me awake—or are they? Is it the other way around? Is my heart consuming this city with dark clouds and rain?

It didn't rain throughout the entire day; it started around suppertime after a threatening afternoon. Under the dark, scudding clouds of late afternoon, my husband and I ducked out the back gate and down the lane for a quick walk. It was a compromise, since a picnic by the river and a long leisurely walk were out of the question under the threatening clouds.

I had a pressing question, and I wanted help from my husband.

My brain seems to fog a little every time I do the math on my own, but for the past few months I've been tracking the time, noting the days are coming closer. My younger daughter is eleven years old, soon to be twelve.

I was nearly twelve when my mom died, but I've never counted the days carefully.

Lately I've tried, but the fog interferes—or is it the rain? I've been finding the darkness of grief unfolding inside—is there a connection, or am I just old and tired enough (and maybe wise, as well) to not press it back into its Box when the sadness starts to mushroom inside? I like to think it is a good thing that I am letting the darkness surface. Perhaps I have learned to trust that my personal Pandora's Box will not destroy my world.

So, today I have this request for help. I ask my husband.

"How many weeks before my twelfth birthday did my mom die, given the two dates?" And the answer surprises me—less than six.

That being so, he recalculates—39 days to be exact. "How close are we to that day in my daughter's life?" I want to know. I know it is close, it has been on my mind, on and off, for two or three months now, this realization that my daughter is the same age I was.

My husband calculates and gives a rough guess, "Around now." I want the exact answer. For some reason the question compels me. He has just said it's close, but on second look, he says, "Well, it's today. Today is exactly 39 days until her 12th birthday."

There is a silence between us for a few minutes as we take this in. I am digesting the surprise that this is the very day in my child's life that corresponds to my own loss—how did I know to ask on this exact day? And I am taking in her age, her level of development—the realization of how far she is from being ready to live without me.

My husband asks if it is fear—the fear that she will not have a mother past this day—that motivates my question. The answer is no. I am no longer afraid I will die and leave my children immobilized by loss. That would have been the reason I did NOT count the days before my first daughter turned twelve. And it would be the reason I did not count the days before I turned 48 (about two years ago) to match my age to the age my mom died. That fear has subsided having been confronted with some medical issues. I feel free to believe I will be here for my girls for a long time to come.

No, it is not fear. It's the reality of seeing my life as a young girl, still very much absorbed in what consumes each day, still very much in need of the tenderness of that bond with a mother. It's about seeing in my daughter the elements of my life that were shattered on this day in my life, 38 years ago.

If life had produced a sieve to catch the shattered pieces of my heart, I think most of them would have slipped through the woven strands, the pieces too small to be gathered.

It is hard for me to imagine, even now, how such a day could be survived by a child. My daughter as that child, or myself as that child.

Yet what I am most sure of is that I survived because I shut the pain off. If it was a faucet, I found the valve and swung it to the fully "off" position, and lived with emotional repression for as long as I possibly could.

I watched a movie last night that included a flashback scene where two children survived the death of their mom. The younger sister was only about seven years old, and the older one might have been closer to my sister's age, around thirteen.

In the movie, the two sisters as adults are no longer emotionally close or supportive of each other. The younger one has sabotaged all her relationships with a lifestyle of alcohol and drug abuse leading to inappropriate and damaging behaviour. But in the flashback, she is a child of seven, her mom has just died, and her older sister puts her arms around her in a comforting hug.

As adults, the older sister admits she didn't give her little sister the support and companionship she needed. For only that one moment, she did hold her, and they clung to each other in their grief. I watch this with the knowledge that I wish for that moment in my life—that moment when I can cling to someone for comfort for the sorrow I feel when I return to the days of loss.

I look back on the day my mom died, the day after she died—which was possibly the worst day of my life, and the day of her memorial service which was another bad day, one of several. I cannot recall a single moment when someone pulled me into their arms and held me in a close, comforting embrace. Of course, the one person I wanted to hold me, the only person that I knew could take me through that pain, was the person causing it—not on purpose, but still, causing it. I desperately wanted my mom's comforting hug, and I only wanted her hug. I can't remember anyone else offering me that tender touch, except for my aunt, whom I barely knew, and who gave me the news.

My aunt who was there had never hugged me before. In that moment of breaking news, she tried to put her arms around me, but the awkward effort of a first hug from her just made me feel worse. So I avoided any further contact with her. Was there anyone who might have held me? I don't know.

I think I was also afraid my tears would melt me. I think in the pain, I felt like a sugar figurine, and the tears, in any quantity, felt like they endangered the continuation of my own personhood. The loss of my mom felt like a crater had eaten my heart and left a gaping exit wound in my chest. I could see I was physically whole, but the pain was so great, it was surprising to see no physical evidence.

In the light of those things—the emotional crater, the physical pain, the sensation of having lost half of myself with the death—tears felt like danger.

I have lived with that discipline for most of my life now. The ratio is terribly unbalanced. Eleven years of emotional safety and 29 years of lockdown on tears. I also have the nine years of healing that have allowed the pain to leak out of my heart in seasons of "weakness." It feels like weakness, but I know that feeling is a traitor to the truth. The tears and sadness are part of the healing, and those are moments of strength, not weakness.

So, now I am in this day—perhaps another day I will never forget. The sun is not shining brightly, the breeze is not pleasant, and this spring day is dark with a storm. The weather has finally caught up with my life.

The sense of what is real is inside my soul: watching my child on this day, when she is exactly the age I was when my world crashed out of orbit. This mess of sadness is like a bale of hay that has been compressed into a thimble in my soul. In part, the hay has managed to slip out from time to time, and healing has begun. But today, there is a bale inside me that I cannot talk about—not even with my husband. It is a choice to let the tears slip out of my eyes.

Today I allow myself to grieve in a somewhat displaced, disconnected way. Today I see myself through the lens of a mother, as the mother of a child exactly the age I was when my mom slipped away. I see my child's needs and acknowledge myself, as a child. I acknowledge my loss with a mother's understanding.

It would be easier, much, much easier, to slip into old habits, and stuff the pain back into the thimble and pretend it didn't need to find its way through my brain, my heart, and my eyes. But I know the road to healing is to let the bale unfold. Even if this process consumes me, it needs to break the many strands that hold my pain captive in a thimble.

So today has been the saddest of Father's Days. I regret that I could not give the gifts of a day of sunshine and laughter to my husband who cares and deserves to be celebrated. But it seems that neither of those (sunshine or laughter, equally) are at my bidding.

Instead, I've given the gift of being real. The real me is still sad, still missing my mom, and starting to wish that I could cry until the tears are a pool big enough to swim in and know that the sadness has escaped my thimble. It seems the thimble should be left ready to catch the rain. But I can't make that happen, and today is not the day for it. Not yet. I cannot even tell my husband about the many things I think when I look back to the year my mom died. The thoughts are locked inside my head, but at least I am letting myself think them. I believe that is good, or at least better than the empty silence.

Today as we walked, he told me that his impression of me was that since the time of my mom's death I have felt alone. I would add one word. I have felt terribly alone. I want to tell him he is right, it is true—I have felt so alone. Until I met him, I felt lost and alone. After we married, I didn't feel lost anymore, but when I wasn't busy with the many things I did to mask the pain, when I let the bale pop a few straggling bits of hay, the words I might use to best describe my pain would inevitably include the word "alone."

These are my reflections for today. This is as much as I can say.

⁂ A Terrible Movie ⁂

. . . . .

⁎ January 2013 ⁎

It is Christmas, and we are in Canada, with a lovely array of options for planning a family night out. We have movie passes that are a gift from an aunt, and we have not seen a movie for a long time. We are all excited about the trip to a "free" movie.

The lines for admission are long, the theatre is crowded, and our wait for tickets eats up half an hour. Our chosen movie is sold out. It is the one we researched, but the kids point out another movie, with a picture of a boy on the poster. He looks about their age.

It's hard to walk away when you have waited this long and have this much anticipation built up for a fun family night out.

Without giving it enough thought, I agree to this, "Sure, why not?" When the movie ends I can tell you at least a dozen reasons why this should have been a "No."

The movie is about the discovery a boy makes, an autistic boy, of his father's death in the crashing towers of 9-11. It is masterfully filmed, the audience unaware that this is his journey until it is too late—you are part of his world and reality, and the pain is intense.

It is searingly real to me, so crushingly familiar that I find myself with tears streaming down my face, but I must keep silence, I must. I cannot tell you what will break if I make a sobbing sound, but something will come apart and be destroyed. There is no trading this truth for any form of comfort, not even a comfort that will break me out of the suspended fiction of the story.

I wrap my arms around my middle and hold myself together. Literally, physically, I hold onto myself, afraid that if I move my arms, even to wipe my dripping nose, my insides will explode. I will no longer be one human, but multiple pieces—again, just like Humpty Dumpty, unable to be repaired. I've gone so far back into my pain that I have forgotten the promises and hope that have come through times of healing prayer. It has not reached all the way into my soul.

My husband notices me and reaches for my hand, but I don't want his touch, and I can't rearrange my survival hug.

I finish the movie in this huddle of arms and heart and soul. I just need everyone to not talk to me or touch me, and I can finish this story. But I can't. I discover I cannot actually finish this story.

The movie ends; there is resolution. The boy who has been stuck alone, isolated by his autism, is finally understood by his mother. His quest for closure, conducted inside the boundaries of his autism, is finally understood. Their connection brings him healing when she finally fathoms his pain and enters his perspective. And I am convinced, in this moment, that this is truly what is healing—that she gets him, that their hearts connect. I am fully convinced that this is where my story differs from his.

I had no one in my years of loss—no one who realized, or acknowledged, or understood what it was that I had lost. No one shared my pain or even recognized that it was still valid when a few years had passed. No one connected in any way that reached me.

As we leave the theatre, this thought is running like a tape inside my head—"no one understood." In my family, we all lived in silent silos, not sharing the deep sorrow we were in. In my twenties I started to talk to my sister about my mom—but never about the pain I felt in losing her. There is a difference.

In this movie, the mother finally understands her son's pain, and this connection heals him. I do not have this in my story—no one has shared and understood my pain. This, I am convinced, is the real tragedy of my loss: I am alone.

My husband, children, and I walk toward a bookshop. My children are running ahead and into the shop, but I sit down on the bench in the mall and tell my husband to go with them and leave me alone.

My husband is in a dilemma. I want him to go, I've told him to go. He knows the kids will be fine, he can stay, he should stay. But I have turned into a stone, not even talking, just saying he should go.

He stays.

He gives me time, sitting beside me, waiting without any unsettling demands. I begin to come to the surface, out of this terrible, dark hole that I have forgotten I live beside, this covered-over abyss.

This is the grief I could not endure and fought to bury the year after my mom died.

This is the consuming darkness that I thought I had overcome with prayer, even prayer for healing of specific wounds. It has cropped up out of the depths, surprising me with how much of my healing efforts have failed to touch the horrible darkness inside Pandora's Box.

When I am able to talk, I tell him the lie I am believing. Or maybe it is the truth; it is just what reality is. But it is not a good place, and he recognizes this as I say it.

"No one understands. No one understands my loss, my pain."

And for once he doesn't think about what to say or take forever to find the "right" thing or talk himself out of saying the wrong thing. Not that those are bad traits, but for once he brings his heart to the table with a simple, frustrated phrase. A phrase that is honest about his part in this journey.

"For twenty years I have been trying to understand. I want to understand. I have no idea what that was like for you, but I want to hear, and I want to understand. You have to let me in, don't shut me out."

And I make the choice that gives me life and hope. I choose to say "yes" to his reality and "no" to the message I took from the movie.

He cannot possibly know what it was like to be me. But if I tell him, he *can* understand or at least connect.

It will take a few years, but yes, he will understand. I am not alone.

⁜ Crackling Voices ⁜

. . . . .

⁜ July 2013 ⁜

My family is in Canada, where we have been for four years. We are getting ready to move back to North Africa. I am grieving leaving my two older kids in Canada, and my heart is heavy and tired. Dealing with grief and sorrow and loss is hard work. But I know that the tears and honest grief are much healthier than a pretence of acceptance and surrender. Still it is not a fun season. It is another loss, and I know that loss is hard, so I refuse to bury it for later. I've had enough of that.

I find a box of cassette tapes packed away, and I look for gems that might have been saved in there. One is exactly that, an old gem. I've found the cassette recording of my mom's memorial service, now forty years old.

I hold my breath and pull on the tape to see if it is ruined by years of lying dormant. It will be a miracle if it still plays and has sound on it. I have never listened to it, and Anna does not even know it exists. It was made for my dad's benefit since the memorial service was held before he got back from Canada, where he buried her in my grandparent's hometown.

The tape is not strong, but it does work, and I put it in the cassette player and gingerly, hope drenching my heart, turn it on. It squeaks and turns and a faint voice is heard. It works. There is a hymn announced and sung and then a prayer. That is all I can stand to hear on the day of this discovery, I feel the waves of memory rising out of my gut and I don't want to face them alone. My sister is coming the next week, and I know she will listen with me.

It is midnight, about a week later. Anna arrived in the middle of the day, but now it is night and we are the only ones up, still talking. Talking until we drop, almost. The house is silent around us. Everyone else is sleeping.

It is far too late to start a new project, but I have waited ten days. As I tell Anna about the cassette, suddenly we both have new energy—we want to hear it! We strain to hear the muffled voices, working hard to identify who is speaking to us from our childhood. Messages of eternal hope on one of the darkest days of our lives—this could wrench us back into the pain. We distract ourselves with the task of identity—sometimes she says the name before I do.

When an old, shaky, withered voice comes on, we both recognize the speaker immediately. We say it in unison. "Mr. Roberts!" She remembers his first words before he says them, she tells me. "He just said, '*Absent from the body, present with the Lord.*' I always remember that." I need to be reminded, these words did not stick to me like they stuck to Anna.

I have only one clear memory from the program of my mom's memorial, it is of "Aunt Betty" singing a hymn with words from Corinthians that she has substituted into the tune. I have that written in my Bible to remember it. Aunt Betty has children our age, but I can't remember any of them being at the memorial service. I don't remember anyone but Anna and I as children in an adult service. The memory of her memorial has sagged a bit with the vagueness that comes to memories over time. Or perhaps it was never very clear. It was a day when the numbness of grief dulled my senses.

The cassette recording of the memorial is long and Anna and I are getting tired having started listening to it at midnight. When the voice of the director begins to give the final sermon, there is a fake, "preachy" tone and vocabulary in his words. "I'm tired," I say. Anna and I agree to stop the tape.

Then she tells me the real reason she does not want to hear Brother Joe. She cannot listen to him, it brings up anger and pain. She tells me a story I have never heard. Once again, we are infused with energy to travel through this new episode, something we have never shared.

On the day of my mother's death, in August of 1973, our uncle and aunt told us the news and prayed with us, and that was all they did and said. I didn't want to be alone, but I surely did not want to be with people I barely knew. Somehow they left my room, and went on with life, it seems.

I stayed in my room, I cannot remember doing anything. But Anna's room was up some stairs, and she was downstairs in the kitchen getting water when the director came over to talk to our uncle and aunt. He must have thought he was doing us all a favour, or maybe he came out of obligation.

Anna waited in the kitchen while the director talked with our uncle, quite normally and jovially...socializing over their visit to Bolivia. Their conversation dragged on for quite a while, in the middle of the house. Finally, just wanting to get to her room, she tried to walk past them. But the director perhaps motivated only by obligation, chose this to say to a 13-year-old girl who had just lost her mother.

"Well, Anna," he began looking at his watch. "Your mother has been in heaven for, let's see, twelve hours now. Isn't that just wonderful?" And Anna tells me it is the jovial tone of his voice and the short burst of laughter making this a joke that hurts her the most. She wants to say, "No, it is not wonderful." But she says nothing as she goes up to her room.

People should say nothing more often, even though that hurts too.

Surely he didn't intentionally mar her memory of this day with this moment of laughter—his jovial effort at lightheartedness. But neither did he have a relationship with us—a history of caring about us. His laughter echoed for years in a chamber of unhappiness where a moment of genuine compassion would have been a salve to a broken young heart.

My sister has carried this hurt inside her silently for forty years. She isn't sure I heard this conversation on the day, and she is right, I did not—God spared me a moment I might not have been able to bear. But she bore it alone, in her own silence, and now finally, she tells me about it. She confesses she has tried to forgive him many times, but she feels bitter and angry whenever she thinks of it. Who can blame her? What kind of man makes an insensitive, pious joke about a death three hours after a girl gets the news that she has lost her mother?

Anna needs me to tell her that what he did was despicable. Not the cartoon caricature of despicable that is in movies, not the kind that ends up resolved with the stupidity realized and redirected into loving kindness. His was a callous, unthinking response—the kind that destroys an inner sanctuary of silence every time she remembers.

So I tell her, and we call it what it is. Wrong. And Anna is no longer alone, she has shared her darkest, ugliest bitterness. And I hope that in this moment of realizing that he was cruel, though he probably never intended to be cruel, she was wronged. He stabbed her wound with a dagger when he could have applied a balm of kindness and compassion. I hope she can now let this go, let God have this offence, and she can be free.

⁂ Red Ruby Cloak ⁂

▪ ▪ ▪ ▪ ▪

My mom has left this world, but she continues to live. My faith embraces the idea that heaven houses her, and I believe I will see her some day, but that is not all. She lives in my memories and is very much a part of who I am, who I have become in my journey to today.

I am grateful for the gift I had of being my mother's daughter for nearly twelve years of my life. If you offered me the choice of having a different mother, someone who would be here in the world with me for longer, I would be in a dilemma, because again and again, I would choose the mother that I was given and lost. But I would never choose the gift of losing her so early in my life.

But it was a gift. In so many ways, it has shaped me and changed my life. It is a gift I don't want and would never wish on someone else, but it has become a precious part of me. While it felt like death broke my heart into a million tiny shards, each of those fragments turned my thoughts to eternity. In a million mundane ways I learned to value what is beyond the obvious. My loss has made me treasure things that I would have missed, overlooked, and lost if I had not received this "gift."

It is part of my healing that I am able to see and value that there is also a treasure in this dark hole of loss. But that doesn't mean I would be able to choose it, and it doesn't mean I am able to say it was "worth it."

Partly, or maybe in whole, I believe this dilemma and the ongoing mystery of never being able to embrace this completely as a gift, is because my human DNA was never intended for a world with death in it. Making sense of the story of Eden has helped me make sense of my life —I understand that I yearn for Eden, for perfection, and every time I encounter life that falls short of that perfection, I am disappointed. Death is the most powerful force that destroys that which I yearn for—the what-was-meant-to-be reality that is broken.

And the story also explains the inner workings of my soul to me. When God put mankind into the perfect garden of Eden, He had in mind that we were there to be connected to Him, made for friendship. When He watched Adam there alone, He observed that solitude was not a good thing, so He made a woman to fit into the crook of Adam's arm. She was the one who shared life at Adam's side. Women were God's invention for companionship. We were made to share life together, sometimes in marriage, always in rich tapestries of relationships and community. When we are taken apart from someone we love, the gap makes a hole, and the hole makes an ache in our soul that reflects our purpose—to be companions. Companions to God and companions to each other.

We have the option to be restored into that companionship with God, in a mysterious-not-quite-fully-understood way. Someday the full-blown version of Eden's friendship, where we meet "in the cool of the day" with God and share face to face, will be restored. For now, we "see dimly, through a veil." And we live in the shadows of a world broken by patterns of sin and loss. Death is part of that loss, and it hurts too much, almost as much as if it is going to kill us, because we were not designed to live with death surrounding us.

Our connection to each other and to God is an element of the healing that is offered through Jesus, the One who reconciles. Through Jesus we can be reconnected to His great love for us. When that happens, God redeems whatever this broken world has dished up for us. In some ways that happens directly through how we relate to God, as a Father who faithfully loves us, but in some ways, that happens through the gift of the relationships we have with people as we journey our way through the life we've been given.

My husband, with his faithful friendship and love for me, has been part of my healing. My children, and the intimacy that grows between two souls that share one body for nine months and then share life for nearly nineteen years, have been healing for me. Anna has continued to share my journey—we are very aware that we share a private, personal loss, and there is understanding between us. And I have friendships that have led to conversations of deep understanding, and care, and forgiveness when things have gone wrong. These also have brought healing to me.

And there have been the powerful times when my imagination has become the Artist's studio, and pictures and scenes have played out in my mind's eye. In this "studio" I have seen something in a new way, and the insights I have been given by the Artist have brought me healing.

There is one scene that has appeared three times in my imagination, each time in a slightly different way.

In a healing session with a psychology teacher at my first college, I was instructed to imagine my mom in a cemetery, with Jesus coming to get her and take her to heaven. If I would release her to Jesus, I was to expect I would find closure that would bring me healing. I struggled to do this, and found it quite difficult, but believed somehow it might help. I am not sure that it did.

The second time I saw this scene, with my mom in a cemetery in the arms of Jesus, sleeping peacefully, I was allowed to refuse the expectation of letting her go, and this was, in fact, far more healing than the first experience.

⁜ May 2013 ⁜

In the third experience of this imaginary scene, I was in a training session for a type of healing prayer that was based on letting Jesus use our imaginations to build a more intimate connection between our spirit and soul, and His presence. It began with a prayer to remember a time when we had felt connected to Jesus in a positive way. While we reflected on that memory, we were invited to verbalize, as if Jesus was sitting across a cafe table with us, what we appreciated about His friendship. We then moved on to an invitation for Jesus to show us His presence in our current context. From there, we opened our inner world of memory and imagination to let Him take us anywhere He wanted us to go—for healing, for understanding, for connection. That connection with Jesus was considered the heart of our life purpose, and the essence of healing.

In this seminar, I began the imaginary visit with Jesus and then asked Him to reveal where He was in my current context. The day before, Jesus had shown me my inner self as a fractured, broken soul. This was no surprise, I live with an awareness of my own brokenness. But what He showed me next was a delightful variation on this theme. My broken pieces were gathered together as if they were all vibrantly-coloured glass, put together in a turning kaleidoscope, creating brilliant, amazing patterns. The patterns kept changing, but the colours stayed the same, and in His hands, I saw my brokenness for something beautiful, redeemed, and worthwhile. Words were redundant to this picture which healed and affirmed me.

On the second day of this seminar, the same colour of red that I'd seen in the kaleidoscope came as part of the image of Jesus. I saw Him near me, wrapped in a cloak made of ruby fragments. The cloak was strong and secure, but actually made of quite small pieces of ruby. So at the same time, it was both shattered and impenetrable. The rubies, together, formed a kind of armour around Jesus and clothed Him in stunning beauty. Then I realized that I was included inside the protection of this cloak, standing by His side, as it surrounded us both.

After I noticed this ruby cloak, I looked up and saw a large jet-black wrought-iron fence, at a distance, all around the perimeter of the cemetery where we stood. Again, Jesus was holding my mom's limp body, asleep in His arms, but I was at His side, feeling quite safe and secure.

From behind the black iron fence, which was not at all ornate, just utilitarian bars keeping intruders at a distance, arrows were being fired toward us. I wondered if Jesus would do something to defeat the enemy and stop this attack. Instead I watched them continue to fly toward us from various directions. I realized that they were going to keep on coming. Jesus seemed happy to ignore them —after all, he was in a ruby cloak of protection.

The danger from the arrows was not threatening or scary in that moment. I knew two things. The effort to wound me with these arrows might never end; stopping the arrows was not the goal. But, equally, I knew that I would be safe from any harm, as long as I was protected by the cloak made of ruby fragments.

My enemies, fear and sorrow and loss, were not going to be removed, but I no longer need worry. I could ignore them and be safe, so long as I was here in the protection offered by this close proximity to Jesus.

Later that day I started the long drive home with a friend who had come with me to the weekend seminar. We drove five hours that day, and arrived to a meeting point with a man, Paul, who is about ten years younger than I am. It was Anna's request that I meet with this family. We met at supper time in the late afternoon. With his teenage daughter, Paul came to get me, and we picked up some pizzas as we started toward their home where his four sons waited for us. As we drove up his road, he asked if I would like to see his wife's grave, and I was happy to do that. So before we took the pizza home, we stopped for me to "meet" her.

As we pulled into a country graveyard, Paul said, "Today is the 15th. She died five months ago today." We sat in his van, and he told me about his wife, what she was like in life and how she had died, the bones of the story.

When we were in his kitchen, unpacking the pizza, he introduced me to his children as a friend, saying that I had lost my mama much the same way they lost theirs, and at a similar age. In fact, the story had several uncanny similarities. This family watched their mother struggle with a vague but not alarming sickness, until just a couple of weeks before her death, when she was diagnosed with cancer.

This family, like mine, lived in a foreign country, and in under a week gathered their belongings and travelled "home" to their passport country, a place where they felt like strangers. That journey was a nightmare, and within a week their mom was admitted to hospital. And suddenly, after 24 hours of crises, fighting for her life, she was gone, much more quickly than Paul was prepared for. The family survived in the waves of shock, living in a fog of slowly realizing this was their new reality, without her. They also had to adapt to being in a new context, with no deep friendships to support them.

The family and I ate pizza and talked. We moved to the living room and talked. We drank tea and talked—until nearly midnight. The littlest brothers had gone back to playing and then to bed, but the three teenaged children sat with their dad in the aging day and told me the whole journey until the horrible last moments had been described. They waited in hope in the hospital corridor, until that final moment of shocking loss—they shared it all with me. I was an utter stranger, yet it was not strange at all.

The biggest surprise came when the kids had gone to bed, the night was clearly done, but Paul had one more thing to say. I met this family because my sister knew them from living in the same country overseas and she asked me to visit them. I had taken a small detour on my trip to spend time with them. It didn't seem like a sacrifice on my part, but I knew it was a significant time.

Paul's gratitude for my visit resonated the themes of my own journey. As he verbalized his thanks, he shared that this was the first time anyone had set foot inside their home to ask them how they were doing. No one from among their friends and church circles had taken the time to come for a visit. And not a single person had made room for them to tell the story of their terrible journey of loss. For him, this was the biggest failure of all. How could a church family live alongside them and not be aware that no one had taken the time to listen?

The next morning we talked about happier memories, still hard to share. Memories of the way their mom made cookies, and the life they had lived overseas, places they visited, normal life—until this traumatic loss. We were friends, sharing an instantly formed friendship, fully trusting each other with our darkest moments.

This stop on a road trip, to spend the night listening and the morning recovering, was the gift I could give, willingly and without reserve. I understood well the loneliness of the months after this loss, and I knew that even one person taking time to validate their pain was important.

Just before noon, we all hopped into their van and drove an hour to meet my friend. The chatting in the van was undemanding—the darkness of the midnight dialogue was behind us, and the sharing of ideas felt like trust had crafted a roadmap for our hearts. I had a thought I wanted to share, but was waiting for the right moment—and as we drove along the highway, it felt like a good time to give my thoughts, the "earnings" of my own journey along the abyss of loss.

I spoke about eternity and told them my theory...a theory that has helped me on several occasions. I believe that God has a trap door in heaven, which He opens from time to time, when we need to know that we are seen in our celebrations or our sorrows. It is so that we can grieve or rejoice more freely, knowing that our lost loved one knows...for this He allows a doorway of connection between our two worlds.

It's not that I think the spirits of the dead are here with us, and it is not a connection I feel in a mystical way. It is just that I know God is merciful, so I choose a theory that gives me comfort. There are days when I believe He has opened the window and said to my mom, "Take a look, child, there she is...your little girl all grown up and getting married." Perhaps because I want to know she is still my mom and part of my biggest days. Or I sense God saying, "Come see this. Your girl is singing to a little girl of her own, she named her after you."

I shared this with Paul's family, in their van as we travelled forward, and then I said the important part— "If your mom was looking through the trapdoor from heaven today, I think she would want me to tell you that she is proud of you. You are caring for each other, and though she never wanted to leave you this way, she is glad you have each other to love. You are doing a good job." There was a catch in my voice as I said it, and then we were all silent together for the next few miles.

When I hopped out of the van and gave each family member a hug, I held them in my arms as best I could, as a mom would do in that brief encounter. I knew it fell short of the comfort that she would have given them, but at least they would not spend a year without a hug that said "I care."

I had considered carefully and prayerfully what I could say to the daughter. I don't know if what I said helped, but I knew it was important that she had met with someone who did not feel awkward talking about the ravaging pain of her mom's death.

Paul's teenage daughter had said less than anyone else during my visit. Her silence spoke loudly into my own soul. The pain of her loss was as tangible as a mist swirling around her, the sadness settled into her face. I knew each day was a tortured journey of missing her mom in a deep, hollow way. I recognized her need for comfort from the very person who had caused this pain. I identified with the anguish of facing the future with no hope of seeing her mom again this side of eternity.

I shared with her an extra few words that I had prayed hard to find—private words, too precious to speak to anyone but her. I had brought her a gift—I wanted to acknowledge that her mother would surely have given her a keepsake gift if she had known she would not wake up the next morning—I knew this as surely as I knew there were two moms in heaven watching us. Perhaps my gift meant nothing, but perhaps it spoke life and words into all the favourite trinkets I know she treasured from her mom's collection of jewelry—I knew this.

I gave this family what my life has taught me. Nothing shakes your world more than the sudden severing of that loving connection between a child and a parent who was always present in your struggles, the ups and the downs that rattle your world while you are still in the vulnerable years of childhood.

But there is a paradox in the gift of having had a parent who was present and loving, and who, now gone, has left a giant hole. Having had their loving connection, they also gave you the inner strength to find your way through the grief. Their legacy is an ability to heal because you were well-loved and connected. In the foundations of their love is the gift that leads to healing and gives you the hope and joy and strength to live again.

Unfortunately, the only way to get back to that gift, to access the joy of that gift, is through the valley of grief. You travel through the pain, the sorrow, the loss, in order to find the gift of rest from the agony. You will probably miss that loved one for the rest of your life, but as you grieve, you come back to the gift of joy that you had them for the time they were here.

⁂ A Green, Happy Place ⁂

▪ ▪ ▪ ▪ ▪

⁎ March 2015 ⁎

Today my son put up our green-checkered hammock on our front porch. He's been waiting to do this for over a year, and all the parts finally came together on a spring day, perhaps arranged by God for my benefit. I have just returned from the weekend where I told my story and poured out my sorrow, and my emotional capacity has changed. With sadness and darkness poured out, there is more room for joy. The hammock brings me to a place of joy.

It is a genuine South American hammock, purchased by a friend on a trip to Brazil, at my request. It is better fabric, and brighter colours than the hammocks from my Bolivian childhood but otherwise remarkably similar. It looks familiar and it gives me a deeper, fuller sense of being "home."

We discuss the options of where to put the second hook, and my son drills the necessary holes and gets it all finished, so he is the first to enjoy the lovely sensation of swinging in it. But he lines his body up with the two edges of fabric and sinks into a "U" shape and says it is hung incorrectly. I explain how to lie in a hammock—with your feet at one edge of the fabric and your head at the other edge, diagonally across it. I can remember the day my dad explained this to me, when I was five years old. My son agrees this is much better, and enjoys his afternoon *siesta* there. When he gets out, it is my turn.

As I relax into the fabric cocoon, I am transported back to some of my earliest childhood memories. I feel like I did when I was five years old and in the jungle. The weather of my memories bears no resemblance to the present. It is early spring and chilly and dry today, whereas in the jungle, where I learned to love the hammock, it was always humid and hot with more mosquitoes to swat than time for swatting.

The sensation of going back in time is purely emotional. It takes me to a happy place, a place where I had no pressures from school. I had not yet started my first year of school. The safety of my inner world was uncluttered by any sense of responsibility. I was young, carefree, and living in the moment—just the way childhood should be.

It is not that my childhood was perfect by any means. We each had our trials, some of them more dramatic than others. One day Anna and I were chased down the mud street by an angry bull, escaping his rage by ducking in to a neighbour's yard. We arrived home a little shaken but more worried we'd be in trouble for breaking a rule by going into the house of someone my parents didn't know.

We had our limited menu with those dreaded mushy bananas. And we didn't live without danger. There was a family of snakes living in front of our house—where else but in the banana grove. Of course snakes love bananas!

We had no furniture in our front living room, but two hammocks did very nicely for the sake of a daily afternoon nap. Why else would you have a room for leisure, if not to nap in? Some nights I would sleep there trying to hide from the hungry mosquitoes. I was surprised to find out that the bats hanging in the ceiling of that room terrified a few of our guests. After a few days of being startled when they left for the jungle at sunset, I got used to them. I was not afraid, as long as my parents told me they weren't dangerous.

Sometimes when my dad had a spare seat in the Cessna, my sister or I would fly along with him, as company. We got used to seeing the muddy rivers snaking through the thick jungle below us. We met many missionary families, and for whatever reason, we met a few of the ranchers as well. I don't know if my dad was delivering supplies to them, but occasionally we would stop in at a ranch, sometimes for lunch. My mom said the richest rancher was probably a German Nazi who had fled after the war. It was the first time I had heard of the Nazis. The jungle of Bolivia would have been an ideal hideout.

Even in the year that we were surrounded by the possibilities of loneliness, deadly snake bites, unanticipated troubles, mysterious ranchers—even in the hardest places, I was happy and content. My contentment came from knowing I was loved and cared for and from being together with the unit where I felt "whole"—my family.

So when I swing in my green hammock in North Africa, I take the time to let the worries of the world sink away, or slide off my shoulders. This hammock is my happy place. The slow, lazy, back-and-forth-motion, takes me back to a year when our lives were simple and trust was as tangible as a commodity—"don't put your hand in that basket."

Life wasn't perfect, but it felt safe and sunny, on the inside.

It isn't an accident that this hammock has been reconnected to my life as part of a healing weekend. I recognize that this is a gift to refill my empty spaces, but I have to see it as a good investment. I should swing in that hammock and let my inner world be recalibrated, like an inner GPS recalculating where I am and which direction I am going. It is an ideal place to be with God "in the cool of the day".

I lie back in my hammock and reflect on my life, the early moments of contentment that I haven't forgotten. I recognize with gratitude that it is unusual to have these memories. Not everyone who has lost big, lived through traumatic change, grieved the black hole of death...not everyone has this "hammock place" in their history, this place where restoration waits. I am "lucky" and I am grateful. I get the feeling that God loves a good hammock as much as I do.

I get the feeling of joy—which is of course, the point of all that heals.

This, too, is a healing gift from God's heart to mine.

⁂ The Artist's Studio ⁂

▪ ▪ ▪ ▪ ▪

Science is a set of predictions which follow the laws and patterns of nature. When you understand these laws, you can predict how things happen—whether a sequence of cause and effect will be set in motion. In science, when you know what you are dealing with, you can control the forces to your advantage, channel power into usefulness.

Art is an expression of what exists, and how you experience it. There is less about art that you can predict, or control, and more that is serendipitous...quite beautiful, in the right setting or context. Of course, you can control art if you are the artist—but in life, more often than not, we are the work of art, not the artist.

For me, healing has been more of an art than a science. When I tried to control or navigate it with a plan, that method was less successful for me. The times when I let my despair surface and made the one choice I had control over—to be vulnerable—those were the times healing was released into my darkness.

But if my healing was a piece of art in progress, I was not the one in control of the process or the colours or the means of healing—at least it has not felt that way over the years. Often I have found such joy in a time of healing that I thought I had plumbed the depth of the pain and been set free of the darkness—for good. And then I found myself, one more time, in a new stage of the journey, walking through a valley I thought I would no longer have to face.

I would describe this journey, this process of healing, as my heart being opened to reveal the artwork, but at the discretion of the Artist's timing. I believe there is an Artist, and He alone knows all that is in both my heart and in my future. I expect that He is aware of how all these things are woven together, and from His perspective, the negative space in the art of my life serves the picture of His work in me. I don't expect I will ever embrace that my loss is "good." This broken world has so many shards that are not what He intended when He created us and put us in the garden He had lovingly made. It was a perfect setting for humans to live in, but the choices made broke the mysterious perfection, and we ended up surrounded by our own brokenness. We are still dealing with the reality of that.

Since I am more of an artist than a scientist, maybe my road to healing has reflected who I am. When I look back and make observations, one of them is that I would not want to try to give someone else instructions on how to heal. We each need to find our own road through the valley of the shadows. Or, as Psalm 84 describes it, we travel the valley of tears, turning it into a valley of springs or wells.

Happy are the people whose strength is in
You, whose hearts are set on pilgrimage.
As they pass through the Valley of Baca, they
make it a source of springwater. CSB

A friend told me that turning a valley of tears into a valley of wells involves a lot of digging. There is not much I am in control of, but when it is time to do the digging, opening the dark spaces, I am willing to do that work.

When I was pregnant for a second time, I went to see a counselor for help with the problem of fear. I had no idea that fear, and anger as well, can both be products or evidence of deeply buried pain. I remember that those visits to the counselor were accompanied by an intense concern about cost, with stress that was not alleviated by an assurance that her "help" was worth what I paid. I don't think it was a good time for me to dig into my pain, and she didn't offer insights that helped me do that. Getting help from a counselor was not a successful strategy for me.

Several counsellors that I met socially (not because I was seeing them as a client) seemed to hone in on the events of my mom's death. It felt to me that as soon as they knew I had experienced the death of a parent at age twelve, their interest in probing this trauma trumped every other conversation. I began to feel like this defined me to them. I didn't feel safe with someone if this loss was going to define me—it felt too much like being sucked back toward the black hole.

So I avoided talking to counselors about my great loss, my carefully guarded Pandora's Box, and perhaps this was a mistake. It seems like there were as many mistakes in my journey as there were even mediocre successes. But somehow, I have still navigated some measure of healing, for which I am entirely grateful. I believe it was God who was pursuing me with healing, not the other way around.

Do I think a good counselor would have helped me? Yes, I do. But the risk of finding one was too big for my pain. It was like a balance point on my scale, and the risk seemed bigger than the pain I was carrying around inside of me. Also, the discomfort of sharing your heart with someone who keeps your story at a professional level and helps you in exchange for money is sometimes too cold for something this deep, this personal. I was not able to cross that barrier, but as luck would have it ... or rather, in God's own good time, the right people came across my path and became a part of my story. They were, inevitably, people with a genuine love and compassion for me as a person, which made them safe and trustworthy.

When I think about my dad and his response to my pain, or his lack of response and connection, I have wondered over the years if he was emotionally deaf. But the closer I am to the age he was, and the better I understand the circumstances of becoming a single parent when my mom died, the more I am aware of his limitations. I am not surprised that he had no idea how to reach into my world. He had not been an emotionally-engaged parent up to the point of my mom's death—she was the one I would talk to about anything that was crouching at the door of my world. My dad was always involved, someone who drove us on adventurous picnics and taught us how to swim. But he never talked about emotional things, before or after her death, and that would have been an impossible learning curve for him to navigate in the midst of his own loss.

As the still-living parent, he made a few obvious mistakes. He told me not to cry, when we should have cried together until we dissolved into a lake of salt, if necessary. He told me to be strong, when strength would have meant the opposite of silence. It would have taken all our courage to talk to each other and expose the pain of the empty spaces inside. My dad never brought up my mom's name. Even on her birthday, a month after mine, we didn't mention a thing. It was as if she didn't exist, and this justified the fear inside of me that she was disappearing from my soul.

But my dad was doing his best, given his life journey, his cultural upbringing and his own needs. In particular, I think the parent of a child who has lost the other parent is at a distinct disadvantage. It must be like living through a crater taking over the place where your life once existed ... maybe even a crater taking over where once a beautiful garden flourished. In the midst of that trauma, you are supposed to figure out how to care for your children who are experiencing a similar crater, probably an even bigger one. The children may have never considered that life could be anything BUT a garden, and now they are in the middle of a sandpit, a sinking sand hole at that.

The personal loss that my dad experienced was tremendous, and his choices reflected his trauma. He didn't do much that helped me, and at times his choices caused harm. But blaming him, or disrespecting his helplessness as he navigated grief, will not help me.

From this long distance, far beyond a few decades later, I have observed with interest times in my dad's life when his journey has been different because he knows the pain of a departure such as this one. Some of the mistakes that affected me have been lessons that were not repeated when others he knew lost a family member. None of that makes it "worthwhile" for me, but it does have value. I treasure the growth I have seen in him.

I've also observed that sometimes when a parent loses their spouse, their own grief overwhelms their ability to be effective in supporting their children through their valley. It is very hard for members of a family to all move through their grief at the same pace. Some family members need distance in order to process their feelings, and others need immediate verbal connection. If people with these two needs are trying to help each other, it is hard for both of them to feel the support they need in a truly terrible situation.

The one thing I have is the choice to allow vulnerability. This much is up to me, and I have learned that when I choose to be honest with my pain, it promotes healing. As hard as it sometimes feels to commit to taking the risk, it is the one thing I can control. Quite often, when I make this choice, the emotional upheaval feels worse instead of better. Letting the pain come up to the surface and then letting it "out" is not fun. The release that comes is often preceded by reliving the hurt. So it takes courage and vulnerability to let that happen, and it can be too scary for some people.

Taking the risk at any cost is not what I am talking about. There are times when trust and openness won't help, when one more harsh judgment might land on me and suffocate my heart. Sharing my inner world with people who don't understand or who actually think they have the answers has been harmful for me. One pastor told me he knew what it was like to lose a parent, that he understood my "problem." He had lost his mother when he was nineteen and just engaged to be married. He reprimanded me for living in the past and told me it was time to move on. Such words are harmful even if shared by a stranger, but coming from a trusted spiritual leader, they leave deep treads in a person's soul and are hard to forget.

I deemed it a mistake to have shared anything about my pain with this man. He had clearly reached a different stage of life than I was in at the time of my mom's death. He was already building a relationship that would lead to a home of his own. He no longer needed his mother the way a child relies on a mother's nurturing love, yet he felt quite confident that he understood my loss and that he had the answer for me.

Both of those elements of confidence—believing that we can fully understand another's loss and that we can somehow make it better, are usually faulty conclusions that signal a disastrous outcome. When we don't listen carefully for what the journey has been to someone else and care about their inner world because it cradles the sacred gift of life, we risk making their pain worse. We can avoid making mistakes that we would rather not have someone else make if we were sharing our deepest needs.

Being willing to listen without the assurance that we will understand is a gift. It feels like we are not doing enough, but it might be the most effective help we can offer. In the act of listening for the details and asking for more explanation, we activate a compassion that validates and cares about how devastating someone's loss felt to them. This often allows a sense of safety, which leads to more openness, allowing more healing.

This interaction between compassionate care through listening, leading to safety and openness, creating room for more honesty, is an active choice. It puts into practice the blessing Jesus spoke of. He said, "Blessed are those who mourn, for they will be comforted." It takes mourning to heal. Without an open, safe place for mourning, our wounds are buried and left to fester. In the tenderness of a truly caring conversation, a sense of sharing sorrow, of being understood and valued, allows the knots of pain unravel and healing to flow.

Being aware that we cannot fix loss, that in fact, we are quite helpless when it comes to healing someone else's soul, is one of the mysteries of healing. Whatever else you say or don't say, comment or don't comment on, one of the keys to hearing about another person's hurt is to know you can't make it make sense for them. Some things are beyond making sense of, and the person who experienced them may never have a comfortable understanding or the feeling it has become a worthwhile lesson. That is not a journey for anyone else to take for them or to push them along.

Compassion, on the other hand, is what we *can* offer a grieving person. Perhaps you have never lost someone truly significant, so you think this can't apply to you. It probably is easier to listen and care if you have gone through something similar, but we all have the capacity to imagine, and in that place of imagining, we can grow deeper as a caring person.

When I reflect on how people reacted to my loss when I was still a child, I remember only one person who actually brought my mom into a conversation. It was a relief to be in the company of an adult who was not afraid to talk to me about her, but we really didn't know each other very well, and it was a short reprieve. In every other conversation and relationship, I felt a reserve at best, and a fear at worst, of the topic of death. People seemed frozen by their concern that they might say something hurtful, and I felt the need to protect them. I needed to skirt the topic and not say something that would cause them to move away from even talking to me.

This was a burden I should not have carried.

I think most grieving people want to be able to talk about the person they loved as if they still matter. If they don't want that conversation, it might be helpful to know why. Any sense of concern that is paired with respect for the loss seems like it would be a welcome gift. But I am only speaking from my own story, knowing that each person's story is different, and needs to be explored as a unique situation, not according to a formula.

That is why I think healing is an art. There is no formulaic answer that will get us to move on from the first stages of shock and wishful thinking to the later stages of acceptance and gratitude for whatever was good before the loss occurred. And the chaos that might characterize the journey between these two phases is anything but predictable—some people even think they are going a little crazy.

But if there are ingredients that I think are important enough to make a list for those wanting to walk that journey with a friend, at least it is a short list. If you are reading this so you can offer support to a hurting friend, I hope you will benefit from these thoughts and advice. These guidelines are the bare essentials of what you might need:

- Listen, listen and listen, more than you talk
- Care with a deep compassion for the brokenness that you imagine might fill someone's whole world
- Don't be afraid; have the courage to stay and be with someone, even if all you can offer is your own silence. And don't be afraid to cry. Sometimes crying together is better than talking.

And if you are a man or woman of faith, put your confidence in the Artist. Know that He created all that we see each day—He has the ability to create yet again. Let Him do His job, and be sure of this—He will do it well. Maybe healing will happen slowly, but it will be a masterpiece when He is done.

⁂ The Maze ⁂

▪ ▪ ▪ ▪ ▪

When my children were preteens we went through a corn maze. I enjoyed the blue sky above us and the gentle rustling of the corn stalks, while my boys loved "the hunt"--they searched for the right answer and remembered the route we had covered. I did not.

As we worked our way through the mistakes that you have to make inside a maze, if you want to get out, I felt lost and helpless. Something in my hidden story surfaced. The maze reminded me of my journey through grief, perhaps--or my journey toward God.

I grew up with an opposite kind of picture in our little church in Cochabamba. It was the "two roads" picture--the road to heaven and the road to hell. One was wide and full of people going toward hell; the other was narrow and sparse, with a heavenly city painted in the far distance. When mom used her expression, "the straight and narrow," I often thought of this picture.

But my own pathway toward God and through this grief that pervaded my life has been anything but "straight and narrow." It has been tricky and convoluted and sometimes even "choked" with a sense of being too difficult for me to discern which way is forward.

The maze is a much better metaphor for my search than the pathway. In a maze, the mistakes you make are both inevitable and useful (though frustrating). You have to turn down a pathway and try it if you want to find your way out--though at least half the time you will hit a wall of futility and realize you cannot get through.

Grief is futility. It is that encounter with loss that you cannot reverse.

And grief is messy. It is more than a mess; it is chaos.

Finding God in my life has been a messy, chaotic, mistake-filled pathway through a maze--and even as I write this, I know I am not "there" yet. Or, I don't think I am. How can I be sure?

A maze that I found most helpful for my own spiritual growth came from Ignatian Spirituality. The discipline of this group of spiritual "fathers" put me in touch with my own imagination in the context of Biblical Scriptures I grew up with. I found a connection to God through reading books and attending Ignatian-based retreats.

The Ignatians have a great regard for both the image of a maze and the use of a labyrinth. At first glance a labyrinth looks like a maze, but it is a circular pathway that winds back and forth until you arrive at the center of the circle formed by the pathway. There are no "dead ends" as you would find in a maze, but there is a lot of turning backwards, in a similar way, that feels like you are retracing your steps. You think and pray as you walk the length of a labyrinth. It takes time and patience to make the journey oh-so-slowly inward.

By walking and praying in this twisting and turning pattern, at times noting that you are walking away from the destination, you have time to reflect. Sometimes those reflections are focused, but other times it is a matter of just walking with patience and determination.

I can easily see that my journey toward healing was similar to walking in a labyrinth. Was working through anger with God part of my maze? I am often asked this question. I have searched my soul for that anger, which I have yet to find--if it is there.

Yes, I was angry. I have no wish to deny that. But not AT God.

Somewhere in my childhood, spoken in a way that did not traumatize or judge me, I heard someone say that all children who lose a parent become very angry with God. I don't know if I heard it before or after the great loss that divided my life into two parts. But I thought about it, and somehow found my way to a conclusion that satisfied me.

The evil in Pandora's Box was not God's evil. If God was responsible for evil, for allowing it into our world, I do not believe it "belonged" to him. Somehow, when the black cloud left Pandora's urn, I knew that there were demons in that force, not God himself.

I chose to blame Satan for my mom's death, and not accuse God. I also had another convenient place to focus my anger. If anger is an inevitable part of grief, mine was concentrated on the person who came into my life as my "new mother." She was not, in fact, a mother to me at all. She became the manager of our home, the teacher of life skills, the force that kept the façade of our family intact. But she was not a mother, nor did she try to be, and so it was easy to blast my fury in her direction. Not openly or violently, but inside my strong walls of silence, I channelled my rage at her. And God took me to the right place to deal with that.

Despite my rage, and at the center of my chaos, God kept hope alive. I credit His presence in my life with the journey that took me toward healing. It was a journey through a maze, not a direct pathway. Times of desperation led to willingness to take risks. Tears led to a profound understanding of worship. Worship led to a connection with God that brought healing, and healing led to forgiveness.

Finding the road to forgiveness, letting go of my stepmother's mistakes and the pain they added to my loss were essential steps in the maze that was my journey toward joy. And this is, I think, the essence of a maze of faith--the journey toward God is inevitably a discovery of joy.

⁂ Treasured ⁂

. . . . .

⁂ 2013 ⁂

When my older daughter started working as a nanny, I offered advice when she asked. Only when she asked. She was in well over her head taking care of two boys, aged one and two, and their big sister who was firmly in charge of the world at the ripe old age of four. It didn't take my daughter long to ask for advice, and so I met the children to observe the situation.

By lunchtime I had my first theory to test. If the middle child, Emerson, was "acting out" due to lack of attention, then feeding him lunch might help. I invited him onto my knee, and he lapped everything up–the food, the conversation, the attention, the love. One-on-one time was the ticket to his heart.

We were soon friends, and despite his fierce tantrums, one of our favourite pastimes was a good snuggle. Snuggle and read, snuggle and swing, snuggle and eat lunch. We had the magic of romance going for us.

It was a love affair where he taught me more than I taught him.

Emerson reacted with obstinate anger to being scolded or disciplined, often repeating the offense to test his boundaries. Sitting on the stairs for a time out sometimes made him more ornery, so I would even snuggle and sit on the stairs with him.

My daughter wasn't sure she liked this plan, but when I explained that I wanted to see if it helped him stay calm and feel safe. She agreed to that.

I had one plumb line: I wanted Emerson to know he was loved. Good, bad, or indifferent behaviour, he was loved. Unwavering, unchanging, unstoppable love. I wanted him to be certain, "This person loves me. All the time."

I began to realize how little I knew about unconditional love. How rarely I had committed to that for my own kids, with this level of intensity and sacrifice. I hoped it was rubbing off—*on me*.

When Emerson threw my glasses across the room and turned around to hit his brother, two misdemeanours in one rage, I picked him up and told myself, "Think fast. This time you have to let him know that this is NOT okay." Still thinking fast, I said, "HELP!" to God. In that interval, my daughter said, "Now what? How is your perfect love going to deal with this?" She admired but was sometimes skeptical of my methods. I'd raised her with a tougher version of love.

I cradled Emerson into my "nook" (the crook of my arm) holding onto him tightly because he was wiggling and wriggling like a boy who knew he was now in trouble. I gave him the familiar snuggle gaze, and looking right into his eyes, I said sweetly but with a listen-to-me-carefully tone: "Emerson, I love you. I love you too much to let you hit your brother or throw my glasses. You cannot do that at my house. Okay?"

And he agreed, "Okay."

And really, love triumphed in us both as I persisted in planting in his heart that he was treasured. When Emerson was impossible, stuck in an angry, negative place, Ama would say, "Come work your magic, Mom." It was a powerful lesson in walking out God's truth. Sometimes he was too stuck to respond, but I knew the love wasn't being wasted. It was just as good for me as it was for him.

And then God began to unravel my heart.

From another century, four decades ago, my own memory of being treasured began to sneak up to the surface.

I was three or four years old the first time this happened. We lived in a community and our "ancient" neighbour (he was about 70) brought me a little packet of candies from the shop across the street. When he put the packet into my hands and I realized it was just for me, I felt like a princess, a royal guest. I felt, in the sphere of this gesture, *treasured*.

Our neighbour, Mr. Roberts, or *Don Robertito* as we called him, would do this from time to time. Just show up with a packet of sweets and put them into my hands. Turns out, I didn't really like the candy. But that moment of receiving the paper packet was so much sweeter than what was inside.

I don't remember that Mr. Roberts spent any time talking to me, certainly no reading together or games or any other interaction. Just a packet of cheap sweets, given occasionally.

And it wasn't that I was the only one he noticed. Mr. Roberts also made a plate of food for a blind beggar every day at noon. He was known around the neighbourhood as a man of generosity and kindness.

During the first months of taking an interest in Emerson, I recalled the memory of the sweets during a time of prayer, while I was dialoguing with God about how He sees me. This conversation took place over several days. Like a pot of soup simmering to perfect flavour, my thoughts were being formed and "reduced." I began to "taste" how much God treasured me through this memory. He was drawing both the thoughts and the feelings forward in my head and heart.

The slow simmering process of daily prayer and waiting brought me to this kernel of understanding: Deep inside me, buried in an old memory, was this sense of being treasured by an old, honourable, generous gentleman.

My ability to feel treasured and delighted in by a father-type wasn't random or accidental or unconnected. It was a deliberate seed, planted in my earliest memories, growing to fruitfulness in this season with Emerson.

That snapshot of myself–the feeling that I am a treasure, that was God's Father heart of love, faithfully deposited into my life by someone who probably had no idea he was doing that. Yet Mr Roberts, my ancient neighbour, knew exactly what the value of a child could and should be.

As I spent days, maybe even weeks, praying this way...reflecting and absorbing the gift, that long ago feeling of being *treasured*...I remembered more and more of the story, with added understanding.

I recalled reading a book about the region we lived in. My candy-packet friend, Mr. Roberts, had lived in a remote jungle village when he was first married. His wife had died there, giving birth to their first baby. Mr. Robert's infant son also failed to survive the complicated birth.

It wasn't the sweet candies that I loved, I didn't even eat them—it was the powerful, magnetic message that I meant enough to him that he would buy that packet and give them just to me. What I felt, as a child, was the message that I was treasured, was a holy gift.

But that message came through Mr. Robert's heart at an incredible cost to him. He knew I was a treasure and passed the truth on to me with power. It was a terribly expensive lesson, for he had paid his own price to be someone who could represent God in my, or anyone else's life.

And then, during these weeks of prayer-soup, it felt like God actually spoke to me. Up until now, my prayers had been more like the "dawning" of understanding—the realization that God wanted me to feel treasured—this was a reflection of His truth and love into my life. I was awakening to the expectation that this feeling of being treasured was God's "normal" for me.

When God spoke, He seemed to say more specifically—"This is what I do. I put a picture of My heart into every child's life. A picture that tells them, 'You are My treasure.' And I leave it there for future reference because I want to bring each one back to that truth some day–no matter how dark their life has been.

"And that is what you are doing for Emerson. You are anchoring him into that love. You will change the course of his life if he gets this."

I knew it was a noble moment. To love an angry, lost little boy until he really understood. Perhaps, it occurred to me, this was the most noble thing I was currently doing with my life. That seemed right.

And then God spoke to me one more time...and one more time after that....Emerson's little brother, Reid, had grown into quite the talker. Reid was the cutest of little boys, with huge, melted-chocolate eyes. He got tons of attention from every direction, including us. There was no reason for my love affair with Emerson to exclude Reid, and loving him together was part of our magic. Love just gets better the more people it touches. So Reid knew he was part of our love circle.

Emerson had now started to attend preschool and was very proud of the friends he had made there. One day just before he turned four, while getting into the van, he announced to Reid, "I have two friends, Mitch and Joey." Reid, the best of little brothers, was not to be outdone. He replied with all pride and confidence, "Well, Ama-mom is ***my*** friend." (Ama-mom is what Reid and Emerson called me).

Reid and I had been playing a senseless game the day before. We were dropping old business cards with stickers on them into a box. He was standing on a stool to make this game exciting. There were no other rules for this game, no "outcomes," and no real sense of accomplishment. It was intended as a speech game for someone else, but we just played it for the fun of watching gravity's relentless hold on old business cards as they drifted down either in or out of the box. As we dropped the cards into the box and watched them fall, we laughed. Endless, senseless fun and laughter, *together*. Joy for no reason other than being together.

And so, for that week, I was Reid's best friend. It was my favourite role of the week: friend to a toddler.

Suddenly it was obvious to me that God gets more joy out of senseless time spent with me than I get from Emerson, Reid, and all my small friends (I have more). This is ***His*** big-time thrill. Almighty and Eternal God, noble in friendship with mere mortals, who have no clue what or Who they've got for their best friend.

And I knew, as clearly as I've ever known a truth: being friends with a toddler was the most God-like thing I could do or be.

To reflect God's love to someone...to let them feel they are a treasure–to plant that anchor in their soul...this is what we were made for.

But to do it well, there may just be an exacting price. So God brought me back around to my memories of Mr. Roberts, this time as I listened with my sister to the cassette tape of my mom's memorial service.

On that tape, I heard for the last time a quavering, old man's voice that I had not heard in over forty years. I knew immediately that it was Mr. Robert's voice, and I loved his message. His words were simple: "Absent from the body, present with the Lord."

I'll remember Mr. Roberts for the two things he planted into my heart. First, he gave me the seed of being treasured, a seed that is slowly growing to maturity, even four decades later.

And second, he spoke truth. When everyone in my world was floundering around me, a child with a broken heart and a crumpled world...when everyone else was trying to avoid the dark or find the right thing to say, he just spoke the truth. No words to explain or justify or qualify her death. Just the simple reality–"She is not here. She is with the Lord."

You can trust a man who has given his life's treasures to God and has lived on with grace and compassion. And you can trust a man who knows the simple truth—someone who knows truth and knows how to step into the costliest moments life holds.

Where there is truth, there is healing and hope. Mr Roberts' life is part of my story of redemption. I bring my dark shadows with me, into community with others. People in pain often recognize that I understand their darkness, but I also carry a torch of hope to walk forward into light.

Nothing, no thing, no time in your life is ever wasted. If you walk in a God-sized dream, there will always be a few nightmares to sort out or wrestle through. But life without a God-sized dream misses the treasure of the moments He fills with His presence. We only see the redemption of our darkest valleys when we let Him lead us to the places He has planned to let us serve at His side, creating treasures where someone else sees only brokenness and loss.

I pray your story will bring you to the full circle of redemption–all you've "paid" in your own soul will come streaming through with the message of hope, wrapped in truth. You will remember and know that your soul is treasured, and you will plant that seed in someone else, to grow there for eternity.

Appendices

Letters

Dear Janet

This is a message I wrote to a friend, on the topic of her friends and their loss. She asked me for some advice, so here is what I sent her. Perhaps it will help you if you have friends in loss and are looking for advice.

Dear Janet,

Thank you for your email yesterday. I love to hear from you, I know you are always interested in what is going on in my life, and I appreciate the way you have of cheering me on. Your friendship is a gift to me.

I am so sorry to hear about the death of your friend, and especially the three children who have been left without their mom. If I understand correctly, it was a sudden death, and they didn't have a chance to say goodbye to her. This makes it extra hard, though, honestly, losing your mom as a child is so hard, I am not sure anything would ever make it easier than just plain impossibly difficult.

How can you understand this journey they are on? You ask for my insights. I am not sure I can explain the pain a child feels in general, I can only tell you about my own story, which I am in the middle of writing, so I will send you some chapters. And from this, you might get some clues as to what your friends' children are having to face, especially because two of them are near the age I was when my mom died. Children who are younger respond quite differently because they don't have the cognitive and emotional maturity to understand life and death yet. But don't think that means the death has less impact on them.

I also feel that to really understand a child's response and needs, you probably have to journey with them for a while. My sister and I had each a very unique perspective on some parts of our shared loss.

What can I tell you that might be helpful? This, again, is probably beyond me. I can only tell you my own set of needs and wishes and the pit I fell into, and you may find that these children have a different way of expressing their needs, and may even reject your wish to be supportive of them. I will say this. There is a good chance that if they feel that your support is part of an obligation, or in any way self-serving, they may cut it off and prefer misery in solitude over having to carry the weight of your need to help them, or your need to process their mother's death.

What does that mean? Well, if they feel a need to help you work out your anger at God for allowing her to die, or if they feel your fear of death, or if your inner motivation is tinged with a need to be a superhero and do something significant with your own resources, they may not want that. Some children are very intuitive, and in my experience, my intuition was heightened by my intense pain, and I was very aware of these attitudes. Maybe I interpreted people's attitudes wrongly, how would I know that? But I did have a sense of being quite clearly able to "feel" what people were projecting, and for the most part, these attitudes often made it harder for me to be honest about my own needs. I also didn't like it when I felt people were grieving "my grief" for me. It was good to hear and know that other people missed her and were grieving her loss for themselves. But at the beginning, I felt weighted down by people feeling this must be hard for me, and their heavy attitude didn't help me. And then it seemed everyone found it easier to move away from the sorrow, maybe moving on, and I was alone. And that was hard too.

What do children want in a situation like this, when a parent has died? This is just my opinion, but probably they want their mom back. And you can't do that for them. So they may want a friend who says, "I just wish I could bring your mom back, but I can't." Then again, that may be the wrong thing to say, I am not sure. There is always the chance you might say the wrong thing, it is a risk. And it is hard for me to define that because it changes from person to person, but I can tell you what NOT to say: You should not try to make this make sense. It does not make sense, in my theological view and philosophical outlook, because Eden was meant to be perfect and we were made to live in that safe Garden. So death just doesn't suit us, it contravenes our very DNA. If you try to make it make sense, and say things that even suggest that— "God works all things for good," or "Someday you will see this was for the best," those comments are salt in the wound. Don't expect anyone who is grieving to want you around if you say things like this. Any advice that you think might help should be carefully considered as part of this category. Too often, advice creates a sense of being misunderstood or even a sense that the giver is trying to fix the problem rather than caring about the person who is in pain. Avoiding advice and majoring on being present in order to care compassionately is, in my experience, the most helpful thing.

Maybe I can give you a variation on that last question that will lead to helpful thinking. Why do we want our mom back when she is gone? Why do kids want their mom even when she is an alcoholic or a drug addict or even just unhealthy? It is the strangest thing that there is such a strong link between a child and their mom that even abusive behaviour will not often sever that wish to be held in her arms, to feel safe for just a moment.

Could it be that there is a little bit of that in-the-womb safety that we still remember and long for from the one who gave it to us first? What did being in the womb give us that makes the link uniquely close between a mom and her child? Here are some of my observations, not from a textbook or a research study, but from my own experience and my heart.

The first thing is constancy— she is the one person in all the world who can and often does make the effort to be there for us whenever we need her. My kids can call me at any time of the day or night, and they do...some of them live in another time zone, and literally I will be glad for that call even if it comes in the middle of the night. Is there any way that you can make it clear to your friends' children that you have a willingness to open your heart to them whenever they are ready to talk to you? That would be the gift of a mom-friend and might help them feel they didn't lose every possibility of being cared for to that degree because their own mama has gone.

Another thing that develops in the womb and seems to never end is the obsessive-type love of a woman that takes an interest in any little detail, even the inconsequential ones. Do you remember seeing your sons for the very first time, and how every toe and the size and shape of each ear and each fingernail was quite fascinating to you? That's mom-love right there. Your friends' children will be missing that feeling that there is one person who is so interested in them that any detail they might choose to bring home with a story from school will be listened to with interest. It doesn't have to be an actual reality to be true, though. Not all moms and not all details and not all stories get that obsessive attention, we all run out of focus energy sooner or later and ignore some of what our kids say. But that won't be the way these children remember their mom. They will remember the moments when she truly listened and cared for each detail, and they will miss that and wish for someone to have that intimate connection to the small things in their life. I don't know how you could possibly express that to them, but reflecting on this thought, that mom-love is attentive to the smallest things, might change your conversations with them.

And I expect they will be missing the everydayness of their mom's presence. There will be a multitude of things that they will start to take note of, by way of their absence. The list will be long and possibly overwhelming. Each day there might be between three and ten new things that they notice that she did or said that are not there anymore. I don't know if you can do anything with this knowledge but perhaps it will make a difference to know this.

Sometimes the everydayness is in the little things that end up being shoulder-to-shoulder experiences. Things like washing dishes next to each other, or driving somewhere in the car together, or just sitting snuggled into each other while you watch a movie. These are moments when a child benefits from a silent closeness, because it is not always about filling the moments with words, but with that feeling, "you are not alone." Being all alone is a huge, scary thing for most children, so finding a way to be together, to feel that connectedness to each other, might be a very important part of healing.

And there will be a fear of forgetting their mom. If you are willing to be a person who is able to talk about her, that will help the children by representing that you are a keeper of the memories. It is always good to know that there is someone else who has memories that they might share or at least will not forget, and so their beloved lost one will not be gone in that way. You might even ask them if they would like you to make a collection of memories of her, or memorabilia (letters she sent to people) from her family and friends. My aunt had a letter that my mom had written that she showed me one time, and that was a special moment. Years later, I asked if I could have it, and she told me she had lost it, she had no idea how. That was hard for me, it was in my mom's handwriting, and it talked about me as a child, and it contained a fragment of my life with her that seemed more precious to me than the photographs. I know my aunt didn't throw it away or purposely lose it, but it was a hard moment, a repeat of the loss. To be the opposite, to be a guardian of memories, that is a gift.

There will also be a guilty feeling that comes when the first day of joy returns and begins to fill up the empty space in their lives. I often hear people speak of this, and it resonates with my experience. Somehow giving a message that joy replacing sorrow is not betrayal is important. If you can say that it might even be what their mom would want if she was able to tell us something now...but how to say that and when to say it to a child in grief? This is hard to know.

And never assume that all is well, that adjustments have been made, and that a smile means life is back to normal. I don't know what you can do with this information, but I can tell you that when my dad got married and people sighed a collective huge sigh of relief, that we were back to being a happy family, the truth was quite the opposite. My misery and pain was hidden behind one more, fairly convincing façade, and the barriers between me and this erroneous observation made me feel so much more alone; it added layers of hurt to what were already too many layers of hurt. People's messages that it was taking me too long to heal were terribly hurtful in those years. Compassionate love may feel like you are going along with misery, but that is a better mistake to make than the opposite—leaving a person feeling alone and not cared for at all.

Perhaps if there is just one thing to remember, it is to somehow make it clear to your friends' children that they are not alone. Being alone is a huge problem for most children. It feels precarious to be alone. And yet, they are alone in too many ways, and that is not something you can fix. But if you can find little ways to send the other message, that they are not alone, it might be the thing that helps them carry on. If you can be a safe enough person, familiar enough, that they feel free to cry in your presence, this is the ultimate gift. Not many people can replace a mom's safety in the presence of sorrowful tears.

Oh, but I am wrong, there is one other thing to remember, too. So two things to remember and to give you a sense of guidance in your relationship with these children—to assure them, "You are not alone, and you are a treasure."

There is no way you can say "You are my treasure," the way their mom said that to them. It just won't have the same impact. I think the strength of that message gets unfurled in those first few moments after birth when you hold your child for the very first time, and you know that what you are holding is the most precious thing in the history of mankind: Life itself. As a mom, holding that child, seeing that face for the first time, there is an unleashing of hormones that is like a drug rush, lifting your feet off the ground. The delight, the joy, the euphoria, when my kids were born, was beyond any other good feeling I had experienced.

It's true, that ecstasy faded as I faced the monotony of day after day and night after night of changing diapers and making meals. But it had worked a magic in my soul that I didn't have the power to undo. My kids were so beyond value to me, and that was established so strongly that even the mundane things of life could not remove the message, the truth, that they are my greatest treasure.

And children know that in a deeply profound way. Deep down, they know that they are a treasure, or if no one tells them they are, it is what they long for in their deepest soul. Most children from a healthy home know that they are their mom's treasure. Perhaps if a child loses their mother in early years of development, a "replacement" mom can step in and become that person in their lives. Adoptive moms certainly do this, often out of a deep longing in their hearts for a child-treasure in their lives. Because I lost my mom at an awkward age, as I entered puberty, I don't believe anyone could have become what she was to me, but especially not someone who didn't see me as a treasure. I think someone could have become a great friend, but I don't think anyone could have replaced her spot in my soul.

Likewise, you cannot be that mom to your friends' children, it just won't be the same as having her presence as a reminder of their value. And that has to be okay with you, because that is not your goal. You can have an equally noble and very appropriate goal that touches them in their pain. You can keep alive the message that they are a treasure. It may be that this is the very best you can give them. You can do some little things, and maybe even some big things, that say to them, "I see you as a treasure."

Or if you see a grandmother or an auntie (or even a pastor) who is trying to be that kind of a person to them, you can be a supporting element in his or her life. If she (the aunt, etc.) at times feels like her efforts are falling into a dark hole of grief, that might be quite normal. And if she or he thinks she is doing nothing of any consequence, a single voice that says, "Don't give up, it may be hard, but it is worth it," may make all the difference. Because this healing can take such a long time, it is important to keep on reminding the caring person that they are making a difference even if they see no "progress." It is a long, slow journey, and for someone who has lost a parent as a child, it may not start until years later.

These are just my thoughts. I don't have answers, but I have experience, so take them for what they are worth. If they don't apply in your situation, feel free to discard them...don't wrestle over what I am saying if your instincts tell you it is wrong for the friends you have been called to journey with. Rely on the Holy Spirit to guide you, and know that my experience is just one journey.

And as the last word, but you know it is not the least...never, never underestimate the power of your prayers. I am sure someone, somewhere was praying for me, and it did make a difference. I had very little going for me in the five years that followed my mom's death, but there is no doubt in my mind that God was on my side—Psalm 34:18 is very clearly a promise for these little ones. "The Lord is close to the brokenhearted and saves those who are crushed in spirit."

I've invested my time in writing this for you today because I believe in you. You are the kind of friend whose interest in my life, whose way of cheering me on, whose delight in my successes, adds up to what a child needs when their life is disintegrating all around them and they don't have the adult tools to first of all grieve, then start to rebuild, then move forward into joy again. It is terribly hard for an adult to navigate that journey, let alone a child. We all need a friend, a faithful friend to walk with us in the hardest times, and I believe you can be that for your friends' children.

With all my heart I bless you to be the hands and feet of God in their lives, giving them even the smallest of light in the darkest of places.

Your friend,
Ellen

Dear Ellen

This is a letter that I would like to receive, if that were to happen, a prototype for people who find themselves in the pages of this book not as the person who lost a parent, but as a friend or relative in close proximity. If, finding yourself there, you wish you had known what to do or how to say something more effectively. It is for people who realize they missed an opportunity to be a blessing to a family in distress. It is a letter for the members of Paul's church family (in the chapter Ruby Red Cloak) to write a version of and send to those children or to Paul.

Or maybe, just maybe, there is a feeling inside you that wants to make sure if you can still help someone that you ignored or "froze" around, you could still do something. The people that listened to my story and brought me the most comfort in my journey were part of a group that met 42 years after my mom's death. That was a long time later, but it was the most meaningful of all the healing "crossroads" that I have had up to this point in my life.

So, the following letter is here for your inspiration. It is not too late, and your words might not be needed for a friend's healing. But they won't be a waste of time, because even if you did nothing that caused more hurt, your care in writing now, will be a gift of kindness. Kindness is always a reflection of the source of all love—God.

I offer this short letter to inspire you, and I am imagining it coming from one of the girls who in their teenage years was hurtful to me. I am imagining that having read this, they realize that they failed to notice that their exclusion of me from their circle of friends was exactly the opposite of the kindness that would have helped. Kindness that would have said, "I know unimaginable sadness has shadowed your life. I care, and I want you to know you are not alone."

Dear Ellen,

I have just read a book on what it might have been like for you to suffer the loss of a parent in your childhood. This book gave me a window into your grief that I had never imagined or thought of. It was an insight that startled me and caused me to regret that I didn't realize how terrible the loss of a parent might be for a child.

I am sure you have thought to yourself many times, "They just don't know what it feels like to lose a parent." And that is true—I just didn't know.

But now that I have some idea of the terrible pain you went through, I wish I would have done more to care for you. I wish I would have asked you about your pain, or about your mom and what you missed about her. I wish I would have taken the time to just sit with you, hold your hand, or hold onto you, when you needed someone to cry with.

And if my absence as a kind friend caused your heart more hurt, or if I said anything that was unloving in those years, I regret it and I want you to know I am truly sorry.

I trust and pray that your journey has brought you through the sorrow. I hope you have found restful places to stop and mourn and find comfort and healing. I pray that you have been blessed with friends who listen and care. And if not, I would like to offer to hear about your mom now, anything you remember and would like to talk about and share, I would be happy to be the one to listen.

Your friend,
Janice

Dear Vincent

This section is in some ways the hardest part for me to write. It is a letter to anyone who has experienced the terrible loss of a beloved one, but by that person's own choice.

Everything up to this point has come straight from my own heart, straight from my years of experience. Now I write for those of you who have maybe read this book and have not found as much solace as I have and who are struggling deeply with a choking thought— "yes, but my mom's absence was her own choice." Whether your mom (or another beloved) left your family for another life (abandoned you), or whether she/he took her own life, it was a choice she/he made. Your loss was at her/his own hands. I cannot imagine how much pain that adds to an impossible sorrow. I cannot find words to even begin to express the despair that must add to a broken heart.

Dear Friend,

I am so sorry that you have endured this unthinkable pain. As you read this page, I want you to know that as I write this, I am praying for you. I am praying over you the promise of Scripture—

God (himself) is close to the broken hearted,
he rescues those whose spirits are
crushed. Psalm 34:18 NLT

Those words are probably salt in the wound, because in grief we rarely feel the nearness of God to our raw and broken hearts. He, the One who made us, didn't create us for this world of death, and so our soul—our thoughts and emotions and will (ability to choose)—shuts down in the face of great loss. Then slowly we begin to thaw and come back to the land of living.

In that time of raw sorrow, we lose the sense that He is near us. We lose the ability to feel anything much but especially the nearness of our Creator.

It is tempting, in that dark place, to begin to believe the lies of the enemy of our soul. It is tempting and easy, to hang on to what seems right, that evil is truth.

(If you are reading about this in this chapter, but are not a person in this place of loss...and if you know of someone who is struggling in this kind of loss, there is your prayer right there. Pray that in that temptation, they will not replace truth with the sorrowful darkness of a lie.)

About the nature of the world, all I can say will not make this terrible grief inside of you make sense. I cannot. Because this is your journey, not mine. Your road to finding the Light again has to be your own. In my own journey, I found God and His faithfulness in places of great sorrow and silence. You need to find that for yourself, I can't explain it to you or do it for you.

But perhaps I can remind you of two things.

The person that left you of their own choosing got lost, completely lost in their sorrow and darkness. They got so lost and so broken and so deep into the pit of despair that they let go of truth, and that is why this hurts like hell. *It is a piece of hell.* The pain you are in is the darkness of hell that has worked itself into this world through someone else's despair that has rammed through your life.

Can I ask you to hang on to God and His love and truth? Nope, I cannot. Your hands are probably too tired to do that.

But can I ask God to hang on to you? Yes, I can and I will. I am asking God to hang on to you today—to hold you in His mercy and grace and tenderness and love and to give you the air you need just to breathe. And I am believing for you, and with you, that God will hold on to you. Just hold you until you are ready to let one finger at a time thaw from this terrible frozen pain you are in.

And can I remind you of one thing? Probably you won't remember it, or won't make sense of it today, so come back here when you have rested in God's big hands for a while and read it again. And again, if you need to.

There was a man named Vincent who drew and painted the most beautiful pictures of the stars in the night. The night was his darkness, and the stars were his belief that there was light out there. And still he took his own life.

But his pictures are breathtaking in beautiful poetry, poetry of the soul on a canvas. He understood beauty and light. Still he failed to find healing, and he let go of his own life.

The reason you hurt so much, so insanely much in this moment in your loss is because something of breathtaking beauty was taken from your life. And the person who took it, chose to take it.

When I look at Vincent Van Gogh's paintings, I realize one thing. His tragedy, his pain, his self-inflicted death, does not extinguish the light of beauty in his art. They are still beauty on canvas. But if he had been in my life, I would not be able to enjoy the beauty for the pain he caused. And that is grief, right there. The terrible pain, the terrible hurt, as long as it resides in your soul, will not allow you to see or enjoy the good that is behind it. And I know the good is there, because if it wasn't, it wouldn't hurt so much to lose it.

The effort it takes to grieve, the work of talking or writing or crying or screaming out the pain, until it is no longer consuming your soul...that is what it takes for you to arrive to the place of mourning. Mourning is when you can just cry, quiet tears of sorrow and pain, tears that acknowledge that this loss hurts. First there is the terribly terrifying grief that rips you apart, then there is the quiet spilling of tears.

The grief is limited, it will take time, but it will end. But the sorrow may not be limited. You may feel this sorrow for the rest of your life, but it will not consume you if you let it lead you to comfort. Every time you sorrow, every time that you shed tears and quietly let the pain of loss out from deep in your soul, you will make more room for the joy that you once had to return.

Mourning is a blessing because it leads to comfort, and comfort leads to remembering what is good. And healing leads to joy in what was there first. You will be able to look at Vincent's painting of the night sky and rejoice in what he saw—beauty.

I promise you two things. God is holding you. God put beauty into the life of the one who is gone, and no matter how distant that feels, there is beauty there. Your journey of mourning will take you back to where you can rejoice in that beauty.

I am guessing you don't know where to start the journey. I can offer my advice, you don't have to take it. Here it is in case you want it.

Don't get out of bed in the morning until you have said these words to God—each and every day. "Abba (Daddy), I am in Your hands. You are holding on to me." If you need to say this as well, then add, "I cannot feel You,

I don't really believe You are holding me, but I choose this as my truth. You are holding on to me."

Let God do the holding on.

And if you have some music that brings your soul back to a place of rest, a song from your childhood, or a singer that meets you in a deep place, then put on that music and take as long as you possibly can to lie down and let the music roll over you like a wave. It may take years, it has taken me 15 years of intentionally allowing healing into my life...and your journey may be longer. If there is any music that you know reaches you deeply, then let that be another place where you lie down to rest, and you say those words again, "Abba, I know You are holding me. (I don't believe it, or feel it, but I choose today to say yes, You are holding me)."

When you are ready, God will bring you someone to talk to, someone with ears to hear you. Ears in their soul. When that person comes, you will need to do the talking; choose to talk. You may need boxes and boxes of tissues, that is okay. Just choose to talk.

That may not come for a while. And right now you may feel very alone and very distant from the joy. Death does that to a person. But this is not the end of your story. Wherever you are in your story, know this:

At least one person has prayed for you. God is on your side.

With all the love God has put in my heart....to yours,

and reminding you that I wrote this because I care about you,

Ellen

References to Scriptures
in order of appearance

Psalm 46:1-3

God is our refuge and strength, a helper
who is always found in times of trouble.
Therefore we will not be afraid, though the
earth trembles and the mountains topple
into the depths of the seas,
though its waters roar and foam and the
mountains quake with its turmoil. CSB

2 Corinthians 5:1-8

For we know that if our temporary, earthly
dwelling is destroyed, we have a building
from God, an eternal dwelling in the heav-
ens, not made with hands.
Indeed, we groan in this body, desiring to
put on our dwelling from heaven
since, when we are clothed, we will not be
found naked
Indeed, we groan while we are in this tent,
burdened as we are, because we do not
want to be unclothed but clothed, so that
mortality may be swallowed up by life.
And the One who prepared us for this very
purpose is God, who gave us the Spirit as
a down payment.

So, we are always confident and know that while we are at home in the body we are away from the Lord.
For we walk by faith, not by sight,
and we are confident and satisfied to be out of the body and at home with the Lord. CSB

Isaiah 43:1-4

But now the Lord who created you, O Israel, says: Don't be afraid, for I have ransomed you; I have called you by name; you are mine. When you go through deep waters and great trouble, I will be with you.
When you go through rivers of difficulty, you will not drown! When you walk through the fire of oppression, you will not be burned up—the flames will not consume you.
For I am the Lord your God, your Saviour, the Holy One of Israel. I gave Egypt and Ethiopia and Seba to Cyrus in exchange for your freedom, as your ransom.
Others died that you might live; I traded their lives for yours because you are precious to me and honoured, and I love you. CSB

2 Corinthians 5:8

Absent from the body, present with the Lord.

Psalm 84:1-12

How lovely is Your dwelling place, Lord of Hosts.

I long and yearn for the courts of the Lord;my heart and flesh cry out for the living God.

Even a sparrow finds a home, and a swallow, a nest for herself where she places her young—near Your altars, Lord of Hosts,my King and my God.

How happy are those who reside in Your house, who praise You continually.Selah

Happy are the people whose strength is in You, whose hearts are set on pilgrimage.

As they pass through the Valley of Baca, they make it a source of springwater; even the autumn rain will cover it with blessings.

They go from strength to strength; each appears before God in Zion.

Lord God of Hosts, hear my prayer; listen, God of Jacob. Selah

Consider our shield, God; look on the face of Your anointed one.

Better a day in Your courts than a thousand anywhere else. I would rather be at the door of the house of my God than to live in the tents of wicked people.

For the Lord God is a sun and shield. The Lord gives grace and glory; He does not withhold the good from those who live with integrity.

Happy is the person who trusts in You, Lord of Hosts! CSB

Psalm 34:18

God (himself) is close to the broken hearted, he rescues those whose spirits are crushed. NLT

Hymns

And Can it Be?

And can it be that I should gain
an int'rest in the Savior's blood?
Died He for me, who caused His pain?
For me, who Him to death pursued?

Amazing love how can it be
that thou, my God, shouldst die for me.
Amazing love how can it be
that thou, my god shouldst die for me.

Long my imprisoned spirit lay
fastbound in sin and nature's night.
Thine eye diffused a quick'ning ray:
I woke the dungeon flamed with light.
My chains fell off, my heart was free,
I rose, went forth, and followed thee.

No condemnation now I dread:
Jesus, and all in Him, is mine.
Alive in Him, my living head,
and clothed in righteousness divine.
Bold I approach th'eternal throne,
and claim the crown, thru Christ my own.
Amazing love how can it be,
that thou, my God, shouldst die for me

His Eye is on the Sparrow
by Civilla D. Martin

Why should I feel discouraged?
Why should the shadows come?
Why should my heart be lonely,
and long for heav'n and home?
When Jesus is my portion?
My constant Friend is He:
His eye is on the sparrow,
and I know He watches me;
His eye is on the sparrow,
and I know He watches me.

I sing because I'm happy,
I sing because I'm free,
For His eye is on the sparrow,
and I know He watches me.

"Let not your heart be troubled,"
His tender word I hear,
And resting on His goodness,
I lose my doubts and fears;
Though by the path He leadeth,
but one step I may see;
His eye is on the sparrow,
and I know He watches me;
His eye is on the sparrow,
and I know He watches me.

Whenever I am tempted,
whenever clouds arise,
When songs give place to sighing,
when hope within me dies,
I draw the closer to Him,
from care He sets me free;
His eye is on the sparrow,
and I know He watches me;
His eye is on the sparrow,
and I know He watches me.

By and by, when I look on His Face
by Grace Reese Adkins

By and by, when I look on His face.
Beautiful face, thorn shadowed face.
By and by, when I look on His face,
I'll wish I had given him more.

By and by when He holds out His hands,
Welcoming hands, nail-pierced hands;
By and by when He holds out His hands,
I'll wish I had given Him more.

More, so much more,
More of my heart than I e're gave before.
By and by when He holds out His hands,
I'll wish I had given Him more.

By and by when I kneel at His feet,
Beautiful feet, nail-riven feet;
By and by when I kneel at His feet,
I'll wish I had given Him more.

More, so much more,
More of my heart than I e're gave before,
By and by when I kneel at His feet,
I'll wish I had given Him more.

Resources

If you have read this book and wish you knew where to find the kind of help I have described, I can recommend the following resources to you:

For prayer that takes you to healing through being connected to Jesus, I was trained by Patti Vellota of Immanuel Prayer. I personally recommend Patti Velotta as a Godly, caring, gentle prayer practitioner, with a vast knowledge of scripture. Here are two websites for the Immanuel prayer I described:

http://www.immanuelapproach.com
http://immanuelpracticum.com/book/pastor-patti-velotta/

The silent retreat that I attended was based in Ignatian principles of spirituality. At various times in my life I have encountered these principles and have always found them to be easy to implement as well as effective in drawing my heart closer to the Father. If you want to learn more about Ignatian spirituality or if you want to try out some of their suggestions, I like this website. You could also find someone in your city if you google local Catholic services. Those trained in this stream of theology and prayer are usually able to pray for healing for wounded hearts in ways similar to what I described. Here is a website to get you started:

http://www.ignatianspirituality.com/what-is-ignatian-spirituality/the-ignatian-way

For more information about the relational retreat that we did which led to me telling my story to a compassionate group of friends, you can go online and read about Intimate Life Ministries. One of many books they carry, but recommended by our friends who ran the retreat is their book, *Intimate Encounters.* You can find more information here:

http://www.greatcommandment.net

About the Author:

Elenita J. (who wishes to remain somewhat anonymous due to the personal nature of this book) grew up juggling three cultures. They merged at points into a multi-faceted culture of not-quite-belonging-anywhere. So when she met and fell in love with "AJ" who wanted to travel and live abroad, it was a good thing. They brought up four children in a small city on the fringe of the Sahara desert where she buried two truck loads of manure in the sandy garden and proceeded to grow flowers in every colour. She currently lives in Canada. Since she is now in the season of growing grandchildren, she is happy to be a part of their lives. She mini-blogs on the topic of children and loss on Facebook at: https://www.facebook.com/His-Eye-is-On-the-Sparrow-by-Elenita-J-433345883675089/

Would you like to review this book? Every review received helps boost sales. If you've read this book, and enjoyed it, **please do help by adding a review**. You can do a review on the Amazon sales page which you can find that here:

https://https://www.amazon.com/His-Eye-Sparrow-Elenita-J-ebook/dp/B071DTWTLF/ or in Canada

https://www.amazon.ca/His-Eye-Sparrow-Elenita-J-ebook/dp/B071DTWTLF/

Or you can add a review on goodreads, here:

https://www.goodreads.com/book/show/35058919-his-eye-is-on-the-sparrow?

55704735R00122

Made in the USA
San Bernardino, CA
05 November 2017